1 First Grade

Teacher Edition

Music Expressions™

COMPLETE TEACHER EDITION (EMC1001)
UPC: 6-54979-05103-9
ISBN: 0-7579-0879-9-90000

TEACHER EDITION, VOLUME I (EMC1001A)
UPC: 6-54979-05104-6
ISBN: 0-7579-0880-2-90000

TEACHER EDITION, VOLUME II (EMC1001B)
UPC: 6-54979-05105-3
ISBN: 0-7579-0881-0-90000

TEACHER EDITION, VOLUME III (EMC1001C)
UPC: 6-54979-05106-0
ISBN: 0-7579-0882-9-90000

TEACHER EDITION, VOLUME IV (EMC1001D)
UPC: 6-54979-05107-7
ISBN: 0-7579-0883-7-90000

BIG BOOK (EMC1002)
UPC: 6-54979-05108-4
ISBN: 0-7579-0884-5-90000

D1368514

Credits

PROJECT CREATORS & COORDINATORS

Robert W. Smith

Susan L. Smith

PROJECT EDITOR

Judith M. Stoehr

AUTHORS

Judith M. Stoehr
Lead Author
Creative Insights
Omaha, Nebraska

June M. Hinckley
Department of Education
Tallahassee, Florida

Darla S. Hanley, Ph.D.
Shenandoah University
Winchester, Virginia

Carolyn C. Minear
Orange County Public Schools
Orlando, Florida

CONTRIBUTING AUTHORS

Timothy S. Brophy, Ph.D.
Assessment Specialist
University of Florida
Gainesville, Florida

Art Williams
Media Specialist
Troy, Alabama

CONSULTANTS

June M. Hinckley
National Standards for the Arts Consultant
Department of Education
Tallahassee, Florida

James Clarke
Fine Art Consultant
Executive Director
Texas Coalition for Quality Arts Education
Houston, Texas

Kathy Robinson
Multicultural Consultant
Eastman School of Music
Rochester, New York

David Peters
Technology Coordinator
University of Indiana
Indianapolis, Indiana

Doug Brasell
Web Site Coordinator
Cairo, Georgia

Artie Almeida
Listening Maps
Bear Lake Elementary School
Apopka, Florida

MULTICULTURAL AMBASSADORS & CONTRIBUTORS

Toshio Akayama
Professor Emeritus
Musashino School of Music
Tokyo, Japan

Gloria Kiester
Professor Emerita
St. Olaf College
Northfield, Minnesota

Kathy Robinson
Eastman School of Music
Rochester, New York

Lynn Schroeder
Rock Springs Elementary
Apopka, Florida

ORCHESTRA

Dr. Michael L. Alexander
Houston, Texas

Dr. Gerald E. Anderson
Los Angeles, California

Kathy DeBarry Brungard
Charlotte, North Carolina

Dr. Sandra Dackow
Trenton, New Jersey

Dr. Anne C. Witt
Arlington, Texas

BAND

Jim Campbell
Lexington, Kentucky

Richard C. Crain
The Woodland, Texas

Linda Gammon
Fairfax, Virginia

Gary Markham
Atlanta, Georgia

Michael Story
Houston, Texas

JAZZ

J. Richard Dunscomb
Atlanta, Georgia

Jose Diaz
Houston, Texas

Dr. Willie L. Hill, Jr.
Amherst, Massachusetts

Jerry Tolson
Louisville, Kentucky

CHORAL

Dr. Darla S. Hanley
Winchester, Virginia

Jim Kimmell
Nashville, Tennessee

Dr. Russ Robinson
Gainesville, Florida

Jerry Tolson
Louisville, Kentucky

CONTRIBUTORS
Pilot and Practicing Teachers:

Kara Bell
Great Falls, Montana

Cheryl Black
Camden, South Carolina

W. Elaine Blocher
Derby, Kansas

Karen Bouton
Graceville, Florida

Patty Brennen
Chesapeake, Virginia

Temetia Creed
Tampa, Florida

Scott T. Evans
Orlando, Florida

Debbie Fahmie
Kissimmee, Florida

David Fox
Oviedo, Florida

Mary Gibson
Maitland, Florida

Claudette Gray
Pittsburgh, Pennsylvania

Lisa Hamer
Moncks Corner, South Carolina

Julie Harmon
North Platte, Nebraska

Jennifer Hartman
Shawnee, Kansas

Elaine Hashem
Penacook, New Hampshire

Mark Hodges
Sumter, South Carolina

Beverly Holl
Los Angeles, California

Grace Jordan
Orlando, Florida

Lyn Koch
Pittsburgh, Pennsylvania

Eunice Marrero
Orlando, Florida

Nancy McBride
Anderson, South Carolina

Kathleen Scott Meske
Los Angeles, California

Deborah Mosier
Bennington, Nebraska

Debi Noel
Eugene, Oregon

Keisha C. Pendergrass
Clover, South Carolina

Teresa Sims
Troy, Alabama

Marjorie Smith
Lutz, Florida

Lisa Stern
Winter Park, Florida

Julie A. Swank
Troy, Ohio

Jane Wall
Wexford, Pennsylvania

Kirsten H. Wilcox
Winchester, Virginia

Leslie A. Wooten
LaGrange, Kentucky

RECORDING

Robert Dingley
Executive Producer

Robert W. Smith
Producer

Jack Lamb
Associate Producer

Kendall Thomsen
Recording Engineer

Andy De Ganahl
Mix Engineer

MUSIC ARRANGING

Robert W. Smith

Michael Story

Jack Bullock

Victor Lopez

Timothy S. Brophy

Don Beattie
Piano Accompaniments

Delayna Beattie
Piano Accompaniments

WARNER BROS. PUBLICATIONS

Fred Anton
CEO

Robert Dingley
Vice President: Education

David Hakim
Vice President: Sales

Andrea Nelson
Vice President: Marketing

Jason Beals
Marketing Coordinator

Dave Olsen
Director: Business Affairs

PRODUCTION

Thom Proctor
Project Manager

Gayle Giese
Production Editor

Bill Galliford
Music Arranging Assistance

Donna Wheeler
Editorial Assistance

Heather Mahone
Editorial Assistance

Susan Buckey
Editorial Assistance

Nadine DeMarco
Text Proofreader

Joy Galliford
Text Proofreader

Nancy Rehm
Senior Art Director

Shawn Martinez
Art Director

Thais Yanes
Big Book Page Layout

Al Nigro
Music Engraving Manager

Mark Young
Music Engraver

Glenda Mikell
Music Engraver

Glyn Dryhurst
Director, Production Services

Hank Fields
Production Coordinator

Sharon Marlow
Production Assistance

Credits cont.

TEACHER EDITION
INTERIOR LAYOUT

InterMedia
A Mad 4 Marketing Company

Margaret Stapleton
Project Director

Marie LaFauci
Senior Artist

ACKNOWLEDGMENTS
Thanks to:

Barbara Zimmerman, President:
BZ/Rights & Permissions, Inc.,
for the work in securing the rights
and permissions for the fine art
and photographs.

Donald Norsworthy, for
photography of Mr. Art and Music
Expressions™ characters.

Steve Palm, Vice President,
Scholastic Marketing Partners,
Scholastic Inc., for marketing
consultation.

Gino Silva, Art Director, Scholastic
Marketing Partners, Scholastic Inc.,
for cover and logo designs.

West Music, for use of
instrument photos.

Adrian Alvarez, for the Spanish
translation of "If You're Happy."

ILLUSTRATION CREDITS
(Big Book page/Teacher Edition page)

01/4. Nancy Rehm
02–03/5. Joe Klucar
04/6. Joe Klucar
05/6. Joe Klucar
06/23. Robert Ramsay
07/23. Robert Ramsay
10/30. Olivia Novak
12/35. Ernesto Ebanks
14/50. Ken Rehm
15/50. Candy Woolley
17/56. Martha Ramirez
18/60. Maria Chenique
20–21/62. Shawn Martinez
22–23/63. Jeannette Aquino
24/69. Thais Yanes
25/83. Robert Ramsay
26/85. Ernesto Ebanks
28/94. Lisa Greene Mane
29/99. Olivia Novak
30–31/100. Olivia Novak
32/101. Lisa Greene Mane
33/108. Robert Ramsay
34/107. Maria Chenique
35/107. Lisa Greene Mane
36/109. Shawn Martinez
37/109. Olivia Novak
38/126. Jeannette Aquino
39/127. Martha Ramirez
40/132. Ernesto Ebanks
41/133. Jeannette Aquino
42/134. Jeannette Aquino
44/141. Jeannette Aquino
45/142. Jeannette Aquino
46/142. Jeannette Aquino
47/148. Martha Ramirez
48/149. Jeannette Aquino
50/155. Lisa Greene Mane
51/156. Candy Woolley
52/160. Martha Ramirez
54–55/168. Jeannette Aquino
56/173. Jeannette Aquino
57/189. Candy Woolley
58/189. Martha Ramirez
60/202. Jeannette Aquino
61/206. Jeannette Aquino
62/208. Robert Ramsay
63/234. Shawn Martinez
64/235. Shawn Martinez

Fine Art Credits

"Sylvia" Possum Trot Doll, c. 1953–72. Black, Calvin (1903–1972) and Ruby Black. Hemphill Collection, Smithsonian American Art Museum, Washington, D.C., USA. Transparency © Smithsonian American Art Museum, Washington, D.C./Art Resource, NY.
> pg. 8 Big Book   pg. 29 Teacher Edition

RAGGEDY ANN is a trademark of Hasbro and is used with permission. © 2003 Hasbro, All Rights Reserved. RAGGEDY ANN was created by Johnny Gruelle.
> pg. 9 Big Book   pg. 30 Teacher Edition

Moonwalk, 1987. Andy Warhol (1928–1987). One from a portfolio of two screenprints on Lenox Museum Board. 38 x 38 in. © 2002 Andy Warhol Foundation for the Visual Arts/ARS, New York, and © 2002 Ronald Feldman Fine Arts, New York. Transparency: © 2002 Ronald Feldman Fine Arts, New York.
> pg. 11 Big Book   pg. 34 Teacher Edition

Breadfrog Teaching the Pigeons, 1978. David Gilhooly (b. 1943). Glazed earthenware with poppy seeds. 11 5/8 x 15 1/8 x 11 in. Mint Museum of Craft + Design, Charlotte, North Carolina. Allan Chasanoff Ceramic Collection. 1997.73.34.
> pg. 13 Big Book   pg. 49 Teacher Edition

Empanadas ("turnovers"). Carmen Lomas Garza. (no date). Gouache painting. 20 x 28 in. © 1991 Carmen Lomas Garza. Transparency photo: Judy Reed.
> pg. 16 Big Book   pg. 54 Teacher Edition

Flags on 57th Street, Winter 1918. (oil on linen) by Frederick Childe Hassam (1859–1935). 94 x 6 3/5 cm. New York Historical Society, New York, USA/Bridgeman Art Library.
> pg. 19 Big Book   pg. 60 Teacher Edition

House: Dots, Hatches, 1999. Jennifer Bartlett. (no date). 23-color silkscreen, signed edition of 150. 38H x 38W in. © Jennifer Bartlett.
> pg. 27 Big Book   pg. 91 Teacher Edition

The Starry Night. 1889. Vincent van Gogh (1853–1890). Oil on canvas, 29 x 36 in. Acquired through the Lillie P. Bliss Bequest. (472.19) Museum of Modern Art, New York, NY, USA. Transparency: © The Museum of Modern Art/Licensed by SCALA/Art Resource, NY.
> pg. 43 Big Book   pg. 135 Teacher Edition

Fourth of July Parade (Arkus no. 28). 1930. John Kane (1860–1934). Oil on canvas, 16 x 14 in. The Sheldon Memorial Art Gallery and Sculpture Garden, University of Nebraska–Lincoln, Lincoln, NE. Courtesy Galerie St. Etienne, New York. Transparency: Sheldon Memorial Art Gallery, University of Nebraska–Lincoln, NAA Collection, Nell Cochrane Woods Memorial.
> pg. 49 Big Book   pg. 154 Teacher Edition

Elephant Charge. 1999. LeRoy Neiman. © LeRoy Neiman, Inc.
> pg. 53 Big Book   pg. 162 Teacher Edition

Dancing Girls. From Porfirianism to the Revolution (Dal Porfirismo a la Revolucion) David Alfaro Siqueiros (1896–1974). Mural. Completed 1964. © Estate of David Alfaro Siqueiros/VAGA, New York/SOMAPP, Mexico. Transparency: Schalkwijk/Art Resource, NY.
> pg. 59 Big Book   pg. 201 Teacher Edition

Contents

VOLUME II

VOLUME III

VOLUME IV

SCOPE & SEQUENCE

Perform

SING

Each student will:

Fundamental:
- Sing alone and with others
- Sing accompanied and unaccompanied
- Develop and expressively perform a varied personal repertoire of songs
- Explore and experience age- and skill level-appropriate melodic and rhythmic patterns
- Sing in a variety of tonalities
- Sing in a variety of rhythmic structures

Developmental:
- Explore expressive speaking and singing voice
- Echo and perform melodic patterns (s, l, m, r, d)
- Sing as a soloist or in unison with others

PLAY

Each student will:

Fundamental:
- Play alone and with others
- Play accompanied and unaccompanied
- Develop and expressively perform a varied personal repertoire of songs
- Explore and experience age- and skill level-appropriate melodic and rhythmic patterns
- Play in a variety of tonalities
- Play in various meters
- Play a variety of instruments

Developmental:
- Explore and experience the difference between rhythm of the words and steady beat
- Echo and perform simple rhythmic patterns (♩ , ♫ , ♪) and (♩ , ⁻)
- Play tonic ostinati on steady beat to accompany melody
- Play simple bordun pattern

MOVE

Each student will:

Fundamental:
- Move alone and with others
- Develop an awareness of body parts leading to the body as a unit in motion
- Experience non-locomotor and locomotor movement
- Progress from personal tempo to external tempo
- Explore and experience age- and skill level-appropriate movements
- Respond to musical, visual, and aural stimuli with movement
- Perform microbeat and macrobeat subdivisions
- Progress from movement to dance

Developmental:
- Imitate/mirror specific movements (formal movement) through imagery, dramatic play, and singing games
- Respond with movement to depict song lyrics and instrumental music
- Experience the steady beat and melodic rhythm with movement
- Explore large and small muscle movements

Respond/Reflect

LISTEN

Each student will:

Fundamental:
- Respond to musical stimuli through a variety of ways
- Discern similarities and differences among musical styles, genres, historical periods, and interpretations
- Recognize and discriminate among sound sources
- Use music terminology to describe musical sound sources, events, and mood

Developmental:
- Explore high/low, tempo, and contrasting form in response to musical stimuli
- Explore simple characteristics of aural examples, such as instrumental or vocal, child voice or adult voice, solo or ensemble, accompanied or unaccompanied
- Experience and respond to a variety of historical and cultural musical styles and genres
- Identify single melodic line with tonic accompaniment
- Identify single melodic line with unpitched accompaniment effects

EVALUATE

Each student will:

Fundamental:
- Apply critical and creative thinking in making musical decisions and evaluations
- Make collaborative musical decisions
- Practice self-assessment

Developmental:
- Explain, using simple vocabulary, personal preferences for music

Create

COMPOSE/ARRANGE

Each student will:

Fundamental:
- Organize sound in ways that are meaningful to him or her
- Organize sound in ways that are meaningful to others
- Demonstrate an understanding of structure, coherence, and organization
- Experience the stages of composing: prewriting, drafting, revising, editing, and publishing

Developmental:
- Explore tone color and sound sources
- Create personal songs with s, l, m and rhythmic pulse

IMPROVISE

Each student will:

Fundamental:
- Organize sounds spontaneously
- Respond musically in context

Developmental:
- Create musical effects and patterns that enhance songs, poems, and stories

Read/Notate

Each student will:

Fundamental:
- Use iconic and traditional notation within the grand staff
- Hear and perform before notating
- Read and write musical symbols and terms

Developmental:
- Stage 1: Read and notate simple melodic patterns (s, m)
- Stage 2: Read and notate simple melodic patterns (s, l, m)
- Read and notate simple rhythmic patterns (♩ , ♫ , ♪ ,‖ ⁞ ,‖)

Connect

Each student will:

Fundamental:
- Recognize that music reflects time, place, and culture
- Understand that music is useful, enriching, and transforming
- Identify how music is essential to the human experience
- Make legitimate cross-curricular connections through content and process

Developmental:
- Experiment with language and music through wordplay, poems, chants, children's literature, and songs
- Experiment with visual art, creative play, and movement to enhance the music-making experience
- Experience characteristics of music of various genres and cultures
- Relate music to time/history and setting

Apply

Each student will:

Fundamental:
- Understand the function of music in society
- Recognize the inherent value of music
- Employ critical thinking and evaluative skills in the music he or she performs, listens to, and creates
- Develop audience etiquette appropriate to the performance environment
- Develop a personal awareness of the impact of music in his or her life

Developmental:
- Discuss the role of music in the child's life and the lives of other children
- Describe personal preferences in music

CURRICULUM MAP

VOLUME I

Lessons 1–4 — READINESS
Sing-along (songs from kindergarten)
New Vocabulary: bell, chant, cymbals, drum,
echo, fast, high, loud, low, lullaby, metal,
rhythm sticks, singing voice, speaking voice,
steady beat, tempo, wood, woodblock

Lesson 5 — SINGING/SPEAKING
Perform and label "ta"
Play unpitched accompaniment

Lesson 6 — STEADY BEAT
Sing and sign "sol-sol-mi"
Play unpitched accompaniment

Lesson 7 — REPEATED TONES
Perform "ta" and "rest"
New Vocabulary: rest, repeated tone

Lesson 8 — REPEATED TONES
Sing and play steady beat ostinato
Read and perform "ta" and "ta rest"
Sing and play pitched accompaniment

Lesson 9 — PHRASE SHAPE
Mirroring phrases
Sing celebration songs
Sing and sign "sol-mi" and "sol-la-sol-mi"
Sing in solo and ensemble settings
New Vocabulary: phrase, solo

VOLUME II

Lesson 10 — MELODIC DIRECTION
Explore upward and downward melodic direction
Sing and sign "sol-mi"
Experience half note
Identify and shape phrases
Move to steady beat
New Vocabulary: downward, march, upward

Lesson 11 — MELODIC DIRECTION
Explore upward and downward melodic direction
Shape phrases
Experience tempo
Draw "sol-mi" on spaces
Maintain steady beat
New Vocabulary: melody, pattern, space note

Lesson 12 — MELODIC DIRECTION
Identify and perform upward, downward,
and repeated tones
Shape phrases
Sing and sign "do"
Draw "sol-mi" on lines and spaces
Sing and march to steady beat

Lesson 13 — SPEAKING/SINGING
Shape phrases
Perform unaccompanied call-and-response
Sing, sign, and read "sol-mi"
Sing and sign "sol-la-sol-mi"
Walk to steady beat

Lesson 14 — STEADY BEAT
Perform unaccompanied call-and-response
Identify different voice types
Sing and sign "do"
Identify phrases
Identify and perform speaking, singing
and repeated tones

Lesson 15 — STEADY BEAT
Accompany chant with rhythmic ostinato
Sing and sign "do" in rhythm of words
Sing, sign, and read "sol-mi-do" and "sol-la-sol-mi"
Read and perform phrases
Read "ta" and "ta rest"
New Vocabulary: march, rhythm

Lesson 16 — MELODIC AND RHYTHMIC PATTERNS
Read and perform patterns of "ta," "ti-ti," and "ta rest"
Perform rhythm of the words
Read repeat sign
Practice audience etiquette
New Vocabulary: repeat sign

Lesson 17 — ASSESSMENT
Sing "sol," "la," and "mi"
Identify melodic direction

Lesson 18 — ASSESSMENT
Discriminate voice types
Identify melodic and rhythmic patterns

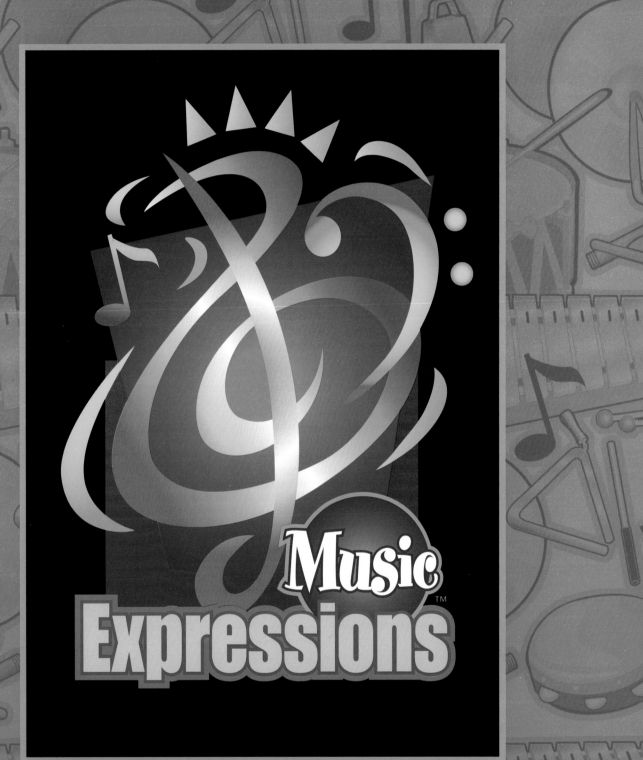

Music
Expressions™

MUSIC

LESSON SNAPSHOT

OBJECTIVES:
- The student will dramatize *The Gingerbread Man* story and *"Gingerbread Man Song."*
- The student will evaluate his or her own performance of *The Gingerbread Man* story and *"Gingerbread Man Song."*

CONTENT	PURPOSE	ACTIVITY	BIG BOOK PAGE #	MEDIA CD*/DVD†	TRACK
"Yankee Doodle"	Review song Maintain steady beat	Review		**CD 8**	**3, 4**
The Gingerbread Man story and "Gingerbread Man Song" Practice and Performance	Practice and perform Videotape performance	Sing Play Move			
Evaluate the Performance	View videotape	Evaluate			
Progress Preview	Assessment	Evaluate performance Teacher observes, listens and records			
"Gingerbread Man Song"	Close the lesson	Sing			

* Tracks shown in green indicate accompaniment tracks. Tracks shown in red indicate practice tracks. These differentiated learning tracks are recorded at a slower tempo to help at-risk and special-needs learners with singing, movement, and language. These are explained within the lessons.

† The DVD is also available in VHS format.

TEACHER REFLECTIONS

INSTRUCTIONAL FRAMEWORK

NATIONAL STANDARDS

- NS1 (Singing)
- NS2 (Playing)
- NS3 (Improvising)
- NS7 (Evaluating)
- NS8 (Making Connections)

CRITICAL THINKING

- Core Thinking Skills:
  Observing, Encoding, Recalling, Setting Goals, Ordering, Representing, Identifying Relationships and Patterns, Elaborating, Restructuring, Establishing Criteria, Verifying

- Bloom's Correlation:
  Knowledge, Comprehension, Application, Analysis, Synthesis, Evaluation

- Critical Thinking Process:
  Synthesis

- Response Type:
  Verbal, Discussion

- Lesson Content Target:
  The Performance of *The Gingerbread Man*

- Thinking Direction:
  Reflection

MUSIC FOR LIFE CATEGORIES

- Music for National Pride
- Music for Other Learning
- Music for Fun and Imagination

CURRICULUM CONNECTIONS

- Language Arts

VOCABULARY

- Steady Beat (review)

ASSESSMENT

- Type:
  Formative, Structured Product

- Assessable Component:
  Evaluation of Own Performance

- Assessment Response Mode:
  Responding

- Tool:
  Worksheet

- Scoring Guide:
  Bi-level, Single Criterion

- Criterion:
  The student evaluates his or her own musical performance

- Levels of Achievement:
  + = demonstrated
  I = not demonstrated

LIFE SKILLS

- Follow Role Assignments
- Identify With Team
- Stay on Task
- Role-Play
- Sense Tone
- Take Turns
- Reach Consensus
- Make Choices

MATERIALS

- Worksheet #9: Character Theme Music*
- Various Rhythm Instruments
- Orff Instruments
- Transparency #8: "Gingerbread Man Song"*
- Worksheet #10 (Assessment): *The Gingerbread Man*
- Simple Props or Masks for Characters
- PR1*

*Transparencies, Worksheets, and the First Grade Progress Record are found in the *Teacher Support Pack*.

EXPRESSIONS

The roots of education are bitter, but the fruit is sweet.

—Aristotle, quoted by Diogenes Laertius

FOCUS THE LESSON

 "Yankee Doodle"
STRAND: Perform: *Sing, Move*

- *Let's warm up our voices today with "Yankee Doodle."*   **CD 8:3**   **CD 8:4**

  Teacher Note "Yankee Doodle" was introduced in Lesson 19.

- Review the song.

- Invite the children to patsch-clap the steady beat as they sing "Yankee Doodle."

DEVELOP THE LESSON

 "The Gingerbread Man" Song Story
STRANDS: Perform: *Sing, Play;*
Respond/Reflect: *Evaluate;*
Read/Notate; Connect

- **Transparency #8:** You may want to review the "Gingerbread Man Song" once again using the transparency created by each class.

- *Today we are going to put all the parts together so we can perform for our parents (or other group). This is called a performance.*

  Teacher Note The purpose of this experience is for the children to be expressive and creative. Do not let the fact that it is a performance detract from that concept. It is more important for the children to be creative than it is for them to have performed perfectly.

- Assign the children to their small groups— the orchestra, the chorus, or the actors.

- Guide the groups as they review and practice all the parts of the music story— the "Gingerbread Man Song," the Character Theme Music on the rhythm instruments, and the running music improvisation on the Orff instruments. (Refer to Worksheet #9: Character Theme Music, if needed.) Provide the chorus and orchestra with music notation, if needed, to assist them in remembering their parts. Use simple props or masks for the characters.

- Practice the entire performance once. Encourage the children to suggest how they might improve their performance.

- Invite other students, parents, or teachers and administrators in the school to be the audience for the final performance of their musical.

  Teacher Note This performance may provide an opportunity to invite parents to visit the school during the day. It may also be something the class could do for a Parent's Night meeting.

- Videotape their performance.

Corresponding Transparency #8

Grade 1 Lesson 25
Transparency #8
"The Gingerbread Man" Song

Use with Teacher Edition, page 166

The Gingerbread Man Song

sol   *mi*

Run, run, run,   fast   as you can.

Can't catch   me, I'm the Gin-ger-bread Man.

© 2002 WARNER BROS. PUBLICATIONS

Corresponding Worksheet #9

First Grade Lessons 26–28
Worksheet #9

Name _____

Classroom Teacher _____

Character Theme Music

Circle your group's character.

Write your group's pattern below.

© 2002 WARNER BROS. PUBLICATIONS

FINISH THE LESSON

3 Evaluate the Performance

STRANDS: Respond/Reflect: *Listen, Evaluate*; **Connect**

- Invite the children to view the videotape of their performance. Congratulate them on their good work.

- *What parts of the musical did you like best? Why?*

- *Which parts would you do differently another time? Why?*

Progress Preview

What:

Are the children able to evaluate their own performance of *The Gingerbread Man*?

How:

1. After you have established criteria for discussing the performance and have viewed the video, tell the children they are going to evaluate (or judge) their performance as a whole.

2. **Worksheet #10 (Assessment):** Give each child a copy of Worksheet #10: *The Gingerbread Man* and a pencil.

3. On their sheet they should write their name, the date, and their teacher's name or classroom number/section.

4. *On the worksheet you will see a face with no mouth. Draw the mouth that best matches how you feel about your performance.* Three expressions are shown on the worksheet as examples. Here is the guide for choosing an expression:

   Smile: I think the performance was great!
   Straight line: I think the performance was okay.
   Frown: I think the performance could have been a lot better.

5. Ask the children to think about their performance and their follow-up discussion and then to draw the mouth that best matches their judgment of the performance.

6. Collect their evaluations.

Teacher Note These evaluations make terrific hall displays.

MARKING THE PR1:

+ = evaluation sheet completed
| = evaluation sheet not completed

③ Corresponding Worksheet #10

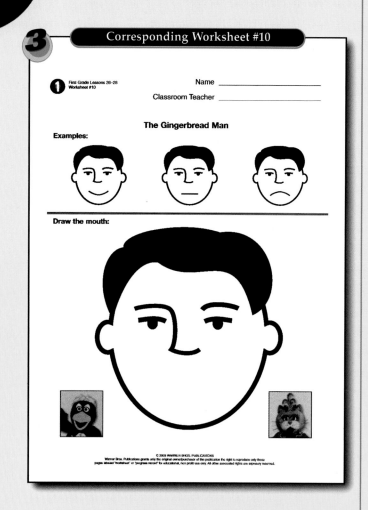

Pause to Think

- *Today we watched and judged our performance of* The Gingerbread Man.

- *Now that we have seen the video, could we have performed the story differently to make it better? Why or why not?*

4 "The Gingerbread Man" Song
STRAND: Perform: *Sing*

- Close the lesson by inviting the children to sing the "Gingerbread Man Song."

28

LESSON

Groups/Categories (combine steady beat and rhythm of the words)

CONCEPTS

LESSON SNAPSHOT

OBJECTIVE: • The student will demonstrate steady beat and the rhythm of the words.

CONTENT	PURPOSE	ACTIVITY	BIG BOOK PAGE #	MEDIA CD*/DVD†	TRACK
"Hello Song"	Wave to steady beat	Sing Move		CD 8	5, 6
"Alley Cat Song"	Move to steady beat	Listen Move		CD 8	7
"Kitty Cat Chant"	Chant and read notation Perform rhythm of the words	Chant Read	57	CD 8	8
"Alley Cat Song"/ "Kitty Cat Chant"	Perform steady beat and rhythm of the words Identify ABA form	Chant Move	58	CD 8	9
Scanning for Progress	Assessment	Distinguish steady beat and rhythm of the words Teacher observes and listens			
"Johnny Works With One Hammer"	Perform rhythm of the words Perform steady beat with partner while singing	Sing Move		CD 8	10, 11
"Goodbye Song"	Perform steady beat while singing	Sing Move		CD 8	12, 13
Literature Extension: *Have You Seen My Cat?*	Explore vocally	Read Speak Sing			

* Tracks shown in green indicate accompaniment tracks. Tracks shown in red indicate practice tracks. These differentiated learning tracks are recorded at a slower tempo to help at-risk and special-needs learners with singing, movement, and language. These are explained within the lessons.

† The DVD is also available in VHS format.

TEACHER REFLECTIONS

INSTRUCTIONAL FRAMEWORK

NATIONAL STANDARDS

- NS1 (Singing)
- NS6 (Listening)
- NS5 (Reading and Notating)

CRITICAL THINKING

- Core Thinking Skills:
  Observing, Encoding, Recalling, Identifying Attributes and Components, Representing, Comparing, Identifying Relationships and Patterns

- Bloom's Correlation:
  Knowledge, Comprehension, Application, Analysis

- Critical Thinking Process:
  Comparison and Contrast

- Response Type:
  Verbal, Discussion

- Lesson Content Target:
  Difference Between Steady Beat and Rhythm of the Words

- Thinking Direction:
  Reflection, Metacognition

MUSIC FOR LIFE CATEGORIES

- Music for Beginnings
- Music for Working
- Music for Fun and Imagination
- Music for the End of the Day

CURRICULUM CONNECTIONS

- Language Arts

VOCABULARY

- Chant (review)
- Steady Beat (review)
- Rhythm (review)

ASSESSMENT

- Type:
  Formative,
  Pre-assessment
  Observation:
  Distinguishing
  Melodic Rhythm
  and Steady Beat

LIFE SKILLS

- Stay on Task
- Work With Partners
- Follow Guidelines

MATERIALS

- Big Book
- PR1*

*The Progress Record is found in the *Teacher Support Pack.*

EXPRESSIONS

[Music] takes us out of the actual and whispers to us dim secrets that startle our wonder as to who we are, and for what, whence, and whereto.

—Ralph Waldo Emerson

Groups/Categories *(combine steady beat and rhythm of the words)*

CONCEPTS

FOCUS THE LESSON

1 "Hello Song"
STRAND: Perform: *Sing, Move*

 Teacher Note The "Hello Song" was introduced in lesson 1.

CD 8:5
CD 8:6

- Sing the "Hello Song" and invite the children to wave to the steady beat as they greet each other.

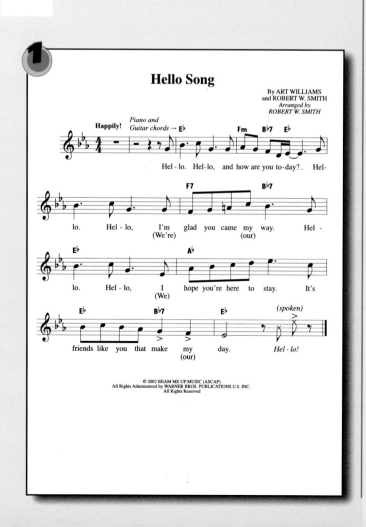

DEVELOP THE LESSON

2 "Alley Cat Song"
 STRANDS: Perform: *Move;*
Respond/Reflect: *Listen;*
Create

- Play a recording of the "Alley Cat Song" and demonstrate the steady beat (macrobeat).

CD 8:7

Teacher Note The macrobeat is the steady beat or heartbeat of the music. The children are not expected to know or use this term.

- Invite the children to maintain the macrobeat by tapping their hands on their knees or desk.

- Vary the placement of the steady beat (to shoulders, back, head, etc.) as the song is sung.

- *The name of this song is the "Alley Cat Song." Find a space in the room where you can stretch your arms to the sides and not touch anyone or anything.*

Teacher Note Free movement exploration allows for expression of creativity.

- Invite the children to pretend to move like a cat any way they choose as long as they do not touch anyone.

Teacher Note To avoid leading their responses, guide the children's movements with role-play or dramatic play by using language and allowing them to respond before demonstrating a movement.

- Remind the children they should move to the steady beat of the music.

3 "Kitty Cat Chant"
STRAND: Perform: *Chant, Move*

- **Big Book:** Speak the "Kitty Cat Chant" while pointing to the notation on page 57.

CD 8:8

- Demonstrate a different voice to reflect the cat's meow each time to add variety.

- Ask the children to clap the rhythm of the words as they speak the chant.

- *Now "think the words" of the chant and clap the rhythm of the words.*

3

Kitty Cat Chant

3

29

LESSON

3 *"Kitty Cat Chant"* Continued

 Teacher Note The ability to "think the words" of the chant in rhythm is a demonstration of inner hearing.

- Repeat the chant once more, speaking and clapping the rhythm of the words.

4 *"Alley Cat Song"* / *"Kitty Cat Chant"*

STRANDS: Perform: *Chant, Move;* **Respond/Reflect:** *Listen*

- Play the recording of the "Alley Cat Song" and maintain the macrobeat during Section A. **CD 8:9**

- Begin chanting and clapping the "Kitty Cat Chant" during Section B, and return to the macrobeat again for Section A.

- *You performed both the steady beat and the rhythm of the words.*

- **Big Book:** Show the ABA form on page 58.

- Play the recording and perform ABA (macrobeat/rhythm of the words/macrobeat) while pointing to the Big Book.

4

189

Groups/Categories (combine steady beat and rhythm of the words)

CONCEPTS

④ **"Alley Cat Song" / "Kitty Cat Chant"** Continued

Scanning for Progress

As the children demonstrate the ABA form of the "Alley Cat Song"/"Kitty Cat Chant" activity, watch closely for those who are having trouble distinguishing between the steady beat and the rhythm of the words. Assist as necessary.

You might want to make a note of any unusual observations on the PR1.

"Johnny Works With One Hammer"

STRAND: Perform: *Sing, Move*

- *The name of this song is "Johnny Works With One Hammer." Teach the song by rote and remind the children to sing with a beautiful singing voice.*

CD 8:10
CD 8:11

- Sing the song to the children and ask them to clap the rhythm of the words.

- *As you sing the song again, pretend you have a hammer and tap to the steady beat.*

- *What is this song about?* (Hammer) *Why do we use hammers?* (To build) *Hammers tap nails to build houses.*

- Instruct the children to find partners.

- *Pretend one of you is the hammer and the other is the house.*

Demonstrate with a child:

The hammer taps the palms of the house's hands (two fists tapping two palms) to the macrobeat as the song is sung.

- Invite the children to sing the song and perform the hammer or house role with their partners.

⑤

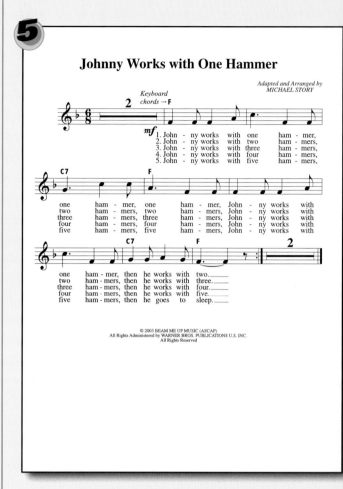

⑤ **"Johnny Works With One Hammer"** Continued

- Change roles and perform again.

- If time permits, ask the children to find new partners and repeat.

FINISH THE LESSON

Recap

- *Today we tapped the steady beat and the rhythm of the words.*

- *Raise your hand to tell me if I am clapping the steady beat or the rhythm of the words.*

It may not be necessary to demonstrate the entire chant or song each time. Perform until a majority of children have their hands raised.

- Demonstrate the "Kitty Cat Chant" with the rhythm of the words and "Johnny Works With One Hammer," first with the rhythm of the words and then with the steady beat.

Pause to Think

- *Today we moved to the steady beat and to the rhythm of the words. You showed me you know the difference between them.*

- *How do you know the difference between the steady beat and the rhythm of the words?*

"Goodbye Song"

STRAND: Perform: *Sing*

The "Goodbye Song" was introduced in Lesson 1.

CD 8:12

CD 8:13

- Close the lesson by all singing the "Goodbye Song." *Tap your pretend hammer to the steady beat as you sing.*

Goodbye Song

By ART WILLIAMS
and ROBERT W. SMITH
Arranged by
ROBERT W. SMITH

Piano and Guitar chords → E♭

Good - bye. Good - bye, to

Fm   B♭7   E♭
you and all our friends. Good - bye. Good - bye, our

F7   B♭7   E♭
time's come to an end. Good - bye. Good - bye, for

A♭   E♭   B♭7   E♭   (spoken)
just a while and then, an - oth - er day we'll meet a - gain. Good - bye.

LESSON EXTENSIONS

Read *Have You Seen My Cat?* by Eric Carle.

Scholastic, Inc. 1987.

Employ vocal exploration with repeated text.

LESSON SNAPSHOT

OBJECTIVES: • The student will demonstrate steady beat and rhythm of the words.
• The student will hear jazz music and recognize its ABA form.

CONTENT	PURPOSE	ACTIVITY	BIG BOOK PAGE #	MEDIA CD*/DVD†	TRACK
"Hello Song"	Move to steady beat with a partner	Sing Move		CD 8	14, 15
"Johnny Works With One Hammer"	Perform rhythm of the words while singing Play steady beat with rhythm instruments	Sing Play		CD 8	16, 17
"Circle 'Round the Zero"	Perform rhythm of the words and steady beat while singing	Sing		CD 8	18, 19 20
"Opus One"	Listen to jazz Recognize ABA form Create movement	Listen Create Move		CD 8	21
Progress Preview	Assessment	Listen Move Identify ABA form Teacher observes and records			
"Goodbye Song"	Perform steady beat while singing	Sing Move		CD 8	22, 23
Extension: Mallet Instruments	Play simple bordun accompaniment with "Circle 'Round the Zero"	Play			

* Tracks shown in green indicate accompaniment tracks. Tracks shown in red indicate practice tracks. These differentiated learning tracks are recorded at a slower tempo to help at-risk and special-needs learners with singing, movement, and language. These are explained within the lessons.

† The DVD is also available in VHS format.

TEACHER REFLECTIONS

INSTRUCTIONAL FRAMEWORK

NATIONAL STANDARDS

- NS1 (Singing)
- NS6 (Listening)
- NS2 (Playing)

CRITICAL THINKING

- Core Thinking Skills:
  Observing, Encoding, Recalling, Identifying Attributes and Components, Representing, Identifying Relationships and Patterns

- Bloom's Correlation:
  Knowledge, Comprehension, Application, Analysis

- Critical Thinking Process:
  Making Connections

- Response Type:
  Verbal, Discussion

- Lesson Content Target:
  Rhythm of the Words and Steady Beat

- Thinking Direction:
  Reflection

MUSIC FOR LIFE CATEGORIES

- Music for Working
- Music to Remember
- Music for Moving
- Music for Beginnings

CURRICULUM CONNECTIONS

- Language Arts

VOCABULARY

- Rhythm (review)
- Steady Beat (review)

ASSESSMENT

- Type:
  Formative, Structured Experience

- Assessable Component:
  Aural Discrimination, Same/Different: ABA Form

- Assessment Response Mode:
  Responding— Performance Demonstration

- Tool:
  Observation

- Scoring Guide:
  Bi-level, Single Criterion

- Criterion:
  The student aurally discriminates between the sections of "Opus One"

- Levels of Achievement:
  + = demonstrated
  I = not demonstrated

LIFE SKILLS

- Stay on Task
- Follow Guidelines

MATERIALS

- 5 Woodblocks
- PR1*

*The Progress Record is found in the *Teacher Support Pack.*

EXPRESSIONS

Music is the only language in which you cannot say a mean or sarcastic thing.

—John Erskine

FOCUS THE LESSON

1 *"Hello Song"*
STRAND: Perform: *Sing, Move*

Teacher Note The "Hello Song" was introduced in Lesson 1.

 CD 8:14
CD 8:15

- Invite the children to form a circle and shake hands with their neighbor to the steady beat (macrobeat) as they sing the "Hello Song."

Teacher Note If the number of children in the class is uneven, you need to step in to become a child's partner.

- Guide the children to turn around to their other neighbor and sing and shake hands again.

DEVELOP THE LESSON

2 *"Johnny Works With One Hammer"*
STRAND: Perform: *Sing, Play, Move*

Teacher Note "Johnny Works With One Hammer" and the hammering motion were introduced in Lesson 29.

CD 8:16
CD 8:17

- Remind the children of the song they learned called "Johnny Works With One Hammer." Invite the children to sing the song and clap the rhythm of the words.

- *Show me how we made pretend hammers with our fists in the last lesson.* All sing the song with one fist tapping the palm of the other hand to the macrobeat.

- Invite one child to the center of the circle to be the first hammer. *As we all sing "Johnny Works With One Hammer," you will tap the woodblock to the steady beat* (macrobeat). Invite the other children to tap their pretend hammers (fists to palms) along with the leader.

- Select a second child to join the first child in the center of the circle and direct him or her to play the second woodblock.

- Repeat, inviting a third, fourth, and then fifth child to the inner circle to sing and play.

2 *"Johnny Works With One Hammer"* Continued

Teacher Note Asking all children to sing and maintain the macrobeat (fist to palm) while the selected children perform in the inner circle will engage all students in this learning experience.

- Repeat with different children as time permits.

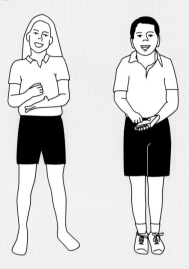

3 *"Circle 'Round the Zero"*
STRAND: Perform: *Sing, Move*

- *Listen as I sing "Circle 'Round the Zero."* Play the recording and clap the steady beat (macrobeat) as you sing.

CD 8:18
CD 8:19
CD 8:20

- *Raise your hand if you can tell me whether I clapped the steady beat* (demonstrate) *or the rhythm of the words* (demonstrate).

- Review the difference between the steady beat and the rhythm of the words.

- Teach the song by rote.

Teacher Note **Practice Track:** The third track of "Circle 'Round the Zero" (CD 8, Track 20) was recorded at a slower tempo to help the children successfully maintain the rhythm of the words as they sing.

- *As you sing the song this time, tap the rhythm of the words on either your knees or your desk.*

- Sing the song again. *As we sing "Circle 'Round the Zero" one last time, you may choose to tap either the rhythm of the words or the steady beat.*

Circle 'Round the Zero

 "Circle 'Round the Zero"
Continued

 Free choice activities provide children with opportunities to express preferences and have ownership in the experience.

- **Mallet Instruments:** To add a simple bordun accompaniment to "Circle 'Round the Zero" using mallet instruments, see "Mallet Instruments" at the end of the lesson.

 "Opus One"
STRANDS: Perform: *Move;* **Respond/Reflect:** *Listen*

- *We are going to hear a piece of music called "Opus One." It is an example of a popular American style of music called jazz. This piece has three parts.* (ABA)   **CD 8:21**

- Invite the children to close their eyes and move their shoulders to the macrobeat on Section A.

 "Opus One" *Continued*

 Asking children to listen with their eyes closed and raise a hand to respond when they hear a change in the music will eliminate peer influence and result in a more accurate representation of what they hear.

- *Listen very carefully and raise your hand when the music changes.* (Section B)

- *What will you do when Section A returns?* (The same as in the first A)

- Play the recording.

- Ask a child to create a movement in place (non-locomotor) to perform for Section A and a movement that travels around the room (locomotor) to perform for Section B.

 You may need to demonstrate two contrasting movements for Section A and Section B and perform them before you ask individual children to create movements.

- Play the recording again and invite the children to perform their movements.

④

Opus One

By SY OLIVER
Arranged by MICHAEL STORY

④ *"Opus One"* Continued

Progress Preview

What:

Can the children aurally identify ABA form in "Opus One"?

How:

1. Ask the children to listen to "Opus One" once with their eyes closed. *Now you are going to show me how well you can tell the difference between the sections of "Opus One."*
2. *Listen again with your eyes closed. When you hear Section A, move your shoulders. When you hear Section B, raise your hands.*
3. Tell them you will write down your observations. If they show the different sections correctly, they will earn a plus (+). If they do not, they will earn a half plus (|). Write these symbols on the board.
4. Play the piece, observe the children, and mark the PR1 accordingly.

MARKING THE PR1:

+ = demonstrates the difference between
Sections A and B
| = does not demonstrate the difference between
Sections A and B

FINISH THE LESSON

⑤ **Recap**

- *Today we tapped the steady beat and the rhythm of the words as we listened to music and sang songs.*

- *Raise your hand to tell me whether I am clapping the steady beat or the rhythm of the words.*

- Demonstrate "Johnny Works With One Hammer" with the rhythm of the words.

- Then clap "Circle 'Round the Zero" first with the rhythm of the words and then with the steady beat.

Pause to Think

- *We sang "Johnny Works With One Hammer" and "Circle 'Round the Zero."*

- *Show me the musical activity we did to both of these songs.* Lead the children to discover that the rhythm of the words and the steady beat were performed in both songs.

6 *"Goodbye Song"*

STRAND: Perform: *Sing, Move*

Teacher Note The "Goodbye Song" was introduced in Lesson 1.

CD 8:22

CD 8:23

- Close the lesson by inviting the children to sing the "Goodbye Song" and shaking hands with a neighbor to the steady beat.

30

LESSON

MALLET INSTRUMENTS

"Circle 'Round the Zero" offers an opportunity to add a simple bordun accompaniment in C pentatonic to the song.

The bordun consists of the pitches low C and the G a fifth above on an alto or bass instrument played simultaneously. The pattern will be:

Will   you   be my friend?

To introduce this:

1. **Prior to the lesson:** Set up a group of xylophones and metallophones by removing all the bars except the C and G for the bordun.

2. Patsch the rhythm pattern of "Will you be my friend"— "ta rest ta rest ta ta ta rest." Invite the children to "catch a ride" with you as soon as they recognize the pattern and patsch it along with you. Ask them to speak the words as they patsch.

3. Instruct the children to patsch the pattern while remaining silent and "thinking" the words "Will you be my friend."

4. When they are comfortable with this, invite the children to sing the song as they patsch the ostinato pattern. Watch for those who can do this easily and select them to play the ostinato pattern at the bass instruments.

5. Encourage the children to practice singing the song as the ostinato players accompany them. **Suggestion:** Play the ostinato twice as an introduction.

6. Switch the instrument players with children who have not yet played. Sing the song again. Follow this pattern until everyone has had a chance to play the bordun while the class sings the song.

LESSON SNAPSHOT

OBJECTIVES: • The student will demonstrate steady beat and rhythm of the words.
• The student will read "sol-sol-la-la-sol-mi" (space/line/space).

CONTENT	PURPOSE	ACTIVITY	BIG BOOK PAGE #	MEDIA CD*/DVD†	TRACK
"Hello Song"	Move to steady beat and phrases	Sing Move		CD 8	24, 25
"Circle 'Round the Zero"	Perform singing game with partner	Sing Move		CD 8	26, 27
"Barnacle Bill"	Sing and sign "sol-la-sol-mi"	Sing Sign		CD 8	28, 29
Artwork: *Dancing Girls* by David Alfaro Siqueiros	Prepare for "Girogirotondo"	Observe	59		
"Girogirotondo"	Sing, sign, and read "sol-sol-la-la-sol-mi"	Sing Sign Read	60	CD 8	30, 31 32
Scanning for Progress	Assessment	Read Sing Sign "sol-sol-la-la-sol-mi" notation Teacher observes and listens			
"Opus One" (Two Recordings)	Review jazz style Identify section changes Identify and perform solo and group	Listen Sing Move		CD 8	33, 34
"Goodbye Song"	Move to steady beat and phrases	Sing Move		CD 8	35, 36
Extension: Mallet Instruments	Play tonic ostinato accompaniment with "Barnacle Bill"	Play			

* Tracks shown in green indicate accompaniment tracks. Tracks shown in red indicate practice tracks. These differentiated learning tracks are recorded at a slower tempo to help at-risk and special-needs learners with singing, movement, and language. These are explained within the lessons.

† The DVD is also available in VHS format.

TEACHER REFLECTIONS

INSTRUCTIONAL FRAMEWORK

NATIONAL STANDARDS

- NS1 (Singing)
- NS6 (Listening)
- NS5 (Reading and Notating)

CRITICAL THINKING

- Core Thinking Skills:
  Observing, Encoding, Recalling, Identifying Attributes and Components, Classifying, and Identifying Relationships and Patterns

- Bloom's Correlation:
  Knowledge, Comprehension, Application, Analysis

- Critical Thinking Process:
  Causal Relationships

- Response Type:
  Verbal, Discussion

- Lesson Content Target:
  "Sol-la-sol" Notation

- Thinking Direction:
  Reflection, Metacognition

MUSIC FOR LIFE CATEGORIES

- Music for Beginnings
- Music to Remember
- Music for Moving
- Music for Fun and Imagination
- Music From Many Nations

CURRICULUM CONNECTIONS

- Language Arts
- Art

VOCABULARY

- Pattern (review)
- Steady Beat (review)
- Rhythm (review)

ASSESSMENT

- Type:
  Pre-assessment
  Observation, Reading
  Notation—"sol-la-sol"

LIFE SKILLS

- Stay on Task
- Make Eye Contact
- Follow Guidelines
- Take Turns

MATERIALS

- Big Book
- PR1*

*The Progress Record is found in the *Teacher Support Pack.*

EXPRESSIONS

It is the best of all trades to make songs, and the second best to sing them.

—Hilaire Belloc

FOCUS

FOCUS THE LESSON

1 "Hello Song"

STRAND: Perform: *Sing, Move*

Teacher Note — The "Hello Song" was introduced in Lesson 1.

CD 8:24
CD 8:25

- Invite the children to form a circle.

- Play the recording of the "Hello Song" and ask the children to shake hands with their neighbor to the steady beat as they listen to the music.

- *Listen to the music again and turn and shake hands with the person on your other side when I say switch.* Ask the children to change partners at the end of each phrase of the music.

DEVELOP THE LESSON

2 "Circle 'Round the Zero"

STRAND: Perform: *Sing, Move*

- Invite the children to sing "Circle 'Round the Zero" with you.

CD 8:26
CD 8:27

Teacher Note — "Circle 'Round the Zero" was introduced in Lesson 30.

- **Play a Game:** *The game for this song is played in a circle. What number looks like a circle?* (Zero)

- **Directions:** Select one child ("It") to walk outside the circle as everyone sings the song.

Back, back, zero

On "back, back, zero": "It" stops behind the person he or she is near.

DEVELOP

2 "Circle 'Round the Zero"
Continued

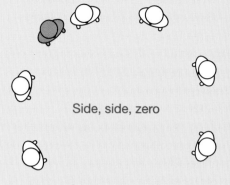

Side, side, zero

On "side, side, zero": "It" stands next to his or her partner.

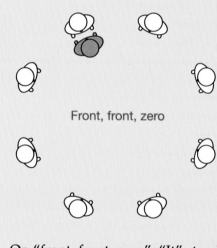

Front, front, zero

On "front, front, zero": "It" stands face to face with his or her partner.

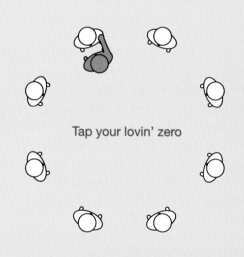

Tap your lovin' zero

On "tap your lovin' zero": "It" taps his or her partner's shoulder to indicate that he or she is the new "It."

- Repeat as time permits.

"Barnacle Bill"

STRAND: Perform: *Sing, Move*

- Invite the children to sing "Barnacle Bill."

CD 8:28

CD 8:29

Teacher Note — "Barnacle Bill" was introduced in Lesson 24.

- Sing the song again, this time adding the "sol-la-sol-mi" hand signs as you sing.

- **Mallet Instruments:** To add a tonic ostinato accompaniment to "Barnacle Bill," see "Mallet Instruments" at the end of the lesson.

- **Big Book:** *Dancing Girls* by David Alfaro Siqueiros. Invite the children to look at the artwork on page 59.

- *What do you think these girls are doing?*

- Tell the children the name of this artwork is *Dancing Girls.*

- *Show me how the girls are moving.*

- *As you dance, pretend you have a large hat on your head.*

---

3 **Corresponding Big Book page 59**

Dancing Girls by David Alfaro Siqueiros

Barnacle Bill

TRADITIONAL
Arranged by MICHAEL STORY

1. When Bar-na-cle Bill was
2. When Bar-na-cle Bill was
3. When Bar-na-cle Bill was
4. When Bar-na-cle Bill was
5. When Bar-na-cle Bill was

one,_____ he learned to play a drum.
two,_____ he learned to buck-le his shoe.
three,_____ he learned to climb a tree.
four,_____ he learned to scrub the floor.
five,_____ he learned to swim and dive.

Bon - nie o - ver in the clo - ver,

Half past one.

"Girogirotondo"

STRANDS: Perform: *Sing;*
Read/Notate: *Melody*

- *"Girogirotondo" is from Italy and is sung in Italian.*

CD 8:30

CD 8:31

CD 8:32

- Play the Language Instruction Track (CD 8, Track 30) and ask the children to echo.

- Teach the song by rote.

- Clap the rhythm of the words while singing the song with the Italian text.

- **Big Book:** Point to page 60. *Look at the Big Book page and find the "sol-sol-la-la-sol-mi" pattern. Where does this pattern occur in our song?* ("Girogirotondo")

- Sing and sign the "sol-sol-la-la-sol-mi" pattern of the word "Girogirotondo" in rhythm ("ti-ti-ti-ti-ta") as you point to the Big Book page.

- Ask a volunteer to point to the pattern in the Big Book as the children sing and sign it.

Girogirotondo
('Round and 'Round)

Italian Folk Song
Arranged by ROBERT W. SMITH

Keyboard chords → C

Gi - ro - gi - ro - ton - do, quan-to e bel-lo il mon - do,

G   G7   C   *Repeat as needed*

guar - da la ter - ra, tut - ti giu per ter - ra.

Lyrics
Girogirotondo,
Quanto e bello il mondo,
Guarda la terra, tutti gui per terra.

Translation
'Round and 'round the circle,
See how wonderful the world is,
Look at the ground, let's all fall down.

Corresponding Big Book page 60

sol sol la la sol mi
Gi-ro-gi-ro-ton-do

---

4 *"Girogirotondo" Continued*

Scanning for Progress

As the children view the Big Book illustration of "sol-sol-la-la-sol-mi" and then sing and sign the pattern, watch for those who may be having difficulty with this task. Assist as necessary.

You may want to make note of any unusual observations on the PR1.

5 *"Opus One"*

 STRANDS: Perform: *Move*;
Respond/Reflect: *Listen*

Teacher Note The children listened to "Opus One" in Lesson 30. The music is shown in Lesson 30.

 CD 8:33
CD 8:34

- Invite the children to form a circle.

- Play the first recording of "Opus One" and ask the children to raise their hand if they remember what this type of music is called. (Jazz)

- *Listen very carefully to Section A and raise your hand when you hear the music change. What do we call this new section? (Section B) When Section A returns, swing your shoulders to the steady beat.*

- *We are going to listen to the same music, except this time you will hear a solo. What is a solo? (One person playing or singing alone)*

- Discuss the difference between a solo and a group.

- Play the second recording of "Opus One" (CD8, Track 34).

- *Listen very carefully. When you hear the solo, hold your hands together. When you hear the group, join hands with your neighbors.*

- Select a child to be the "soloist." Ask him or her to go to the center of the circle and create a non-locomotor movement to perform during the solo (Section A). Encourage the child to move to the steady beat.

- Invite all the children to "groove" to the music while the "soloist" is performing. *Watch the leader carefully, because during the group music (Section B) you must copy the movements he or she created during the solo.*

- Identify a new "soloist" to create a movement and repeat.

FINISH THE LESSON

6 Recap

- *Today we sang a song from Italy that had this pattern in it. Sing and sign "sol-sol-la-la-sol-mi" and ask the children to imitate you.*

- *We also listened to music that had a soloist and a group playing. Which word is the name for one person playing alone, "solo" or "group"? (Solo)*

Pause to Think

- *We read the "sol-sol-la-la-sol-mi" pattern in "Girogirotondo" that was written in our Big Book.* Review the Big Book page 60.

- *How do the notes show you what to sing?*

- *What on the Big Book page matches the way you sing the pattern?*

---

7 "Goodbye Song"
STRAND: Perform: *Sing*

Teacher Note The "Goodbye Song" was introduced in Lesson 1.

(CD 8:35)
(CD 8:36)

- Close the lesson by inviting the children to sing the "Goodbye Song" and shaking hands with a neighbor to the macrobeat of the music.

- *Sing and switch partners as we did with our "Hello Song." I will tell you when to switch.* Provide the oral cue at the end of each phrase of the song.

MALLET INSTRUMENTS

The reintroduction of "Barnacle Bill" in this lesson offers the opportunity to review and perform the tonic ostinato accompaniment learned in Lesson 25. The instructions for introducing this bordun are reprinted here.

1. Set up the instruments in F pentatonic (removing the E and B). Also remove the G bars to isolate the F bar.

2. On the board, write the following two-measure rhythm in 4/4:

3. Ask the children to use their "two-finger clap" to quietly practice this rhythm by reading the board.

Teacher Note A two-finger clap is a quiet way for the children to practice reading rhythms in large groups. They simply use one finger on each hand instead of the entire hand to clap.

4. After about 60 seconds, ask the children to use their full clap to play this rhythm.

Teacher Note Don't forget to "turn" the half note claps—that is, bring the hands together for the first beat, and leave the hands together for the second beat, turning them one-quarter turn. This gives the physical sensation of the two beats without an additional sound.

5. Once they have read and know the rhythm, invite the children to pick up their mallets. Invite the children to play this pattern on the F bar only. Repeat the pattern until everyone can play this on their instruments.

6. Ask the bass instruments and the contrabass bar F to play this pattern as an ostinato while the others sing the song. Change players for each song performance, giving as many children as possible the opportunity to accompany the class.

31

LESSON

LESSON SNAPSHOT

OBJECTIVES:
- The student will demonstrate steady beat and rhythm of the words.
- The student will read "sol-sol-la-la-sol-mi" (line/space/line).

CONTENT	PURPOSE	ACTIVITY	BIG BOOK PAGE #	MEDIA CD*/DVD†	TRACK
"Hello Song"	Move to steady beat Respond to phrases	Listen Move		CD 9	1, 2
"Girogirotondo"	Sing, sign, and read "sol-sol-la-la-sol-mi" (line/space/line) Perform singing game	Read Sing Move	61	CD 9	3, 4, 5
"Jim Along Josie"	Play bordun on mallet instruments	Sing Play		CD 9	6, 7
Progress Preview	Assessment	Demonstrate steady beat Teacher observes, listens and records			
"Over in the Meadow"	Perform rhythm of the words and steady beat while singing and playing rhythm sticks	Sing Play	62	CD 9	8, 9
"Goodbye Song"	Move to steady beat Respond to phrases	Sing Move		CD 9	10, 11
Literature Extension: *Over in the Meadow*	Sing story using traditional tune	Read Sing			

* Tracks shown in green indicate accompaniment tracks. Tracks shown in red indicate practice tracks. These differentiated learning tracks are recorded at a slower tempo to help at-risk and special-needs learners with singing, movement, and language. These are explained within the lessons.

† The DVD is also available in VHS format.

TEACHER REFLECTIONS

INSTRUCTIONAL FRAMEWORK

NATIONAL STANDARDS

- NS1 (Singing)
- NS2 (Playing)
- NS5 (Reading and Notating)
- NS6 (Listening)

CRITICAL THINKING

- Core Thinking Skills:
  Observing, Encoding, Recalling, Identifying Attributes and Components, Comparing, Representing, Identifying Relationships and Patterns

- Bloom's Correlation:
  Knowledge, Comprehension, Application, Analysis

- Critical Thinking Process:
  Metacognition

- Response Type:
  Verbal, Discussion

- Lesson Content Target:
  Steady Beat and Rhythm of the Words

- Thinking Direction:
  Metacognition

MUSIC FOR LIFE CATEGORIES

- Music From Many Nations
- Music for Fun and Imagination
- Music for Nature
- Music for Beginnings

CURRICULUM CONNECTIONS

- Language Arts
- Science
- Math

VOCABULARY

- Bells (review)
- Rhythm (review)
- Rhythm Sticks (review)
- Steady Beat (review)

ASSESSMENT

- Type:
  Summative, Structured Experience

- Assessable Component:
  Enabling Competency:
  Steady Beat

- Assessment Response Mode:
  Performance

- Tool:
  Observation

- Scoring Guide:
  Bi-level, Single Criterion

- Criterion:
  The student consistently demonstrates the steady beat

- Levels of Achievement:
  + = demonstrated
  | = not demonstrated

LIFE SKILLS

- Stay on Task
- Follow Guidelines
- Take Turns

MATERIALS

- Big Book
- Rhythm Sticks
- PR1*
- Orff Instruments (D and A bars) or Resonator Bells (D and A)

*The Progress Record is found in the *Teacher Support Pack.*

EXPRESSIONS

Composers should write tunes that chauffeurs and errand boys can whistle.

—Sir Thomas Beecham

FOCUS THE LESSON

1 *"Hello Song"*

 STRANDS: Perform: *Move*; **Respond/Reflect:** *Listen*

Teacher Note — "Hello Song" was introduced in Lesson 1.

CD 9:1
CD 9:2

- Invite the children to form a circle.

- Play the recording of the "Hello Song" and ask the children to shake hands with their neighbor to the steady beat as they listen to the music.

- *Let the music tell you when to turn and shake hands with the person on your other side. Provide an oral cue if the children do not switch at the end of each phrase of the music.*

DEVELOP THE LESSON

2 *"Girogirotondo"*

STRANDS: Perform: *Sing, Move*; **Read/Notate**

Teacher Note — "Girogirotondo" was introduced in Lesson 31.

CD 9:3
CD 9:4
CD 9:5

- Invite the children to sing "Girogirotondo."

Teacher Note — **Practice Track:** The third track of "Girogirotondo" (CD 9, Track 5) was recorded at a slower tempo to help the children practice the Italian language and perform the rhythm of the words.

- **Big Book:** Show page 61 and ask the children to find the "sol-sol-la-la-sol-mi" pattern.

Teacher Note — It may be necessary to show the Big Book page 60 of this song again to compare the "sol-sol-la-la-sol-mi" patterns (beginning on a space or beginning on a line).

2 Corresponding Big Book page 61

sol sol la la sol mi
Gi-ro - gi - ro-ton-do

2 *"Girogirotondo"* Continued

- Sing and sign a "sol-sol-la-la-sol-mi" pattern.

- *How is this "sol-sol-la-la-sol-mi" pattern different from the "sol-sol-la-la-sol-mi" pattern we read in the last lesson? (This "sol-sol-la-la-sol-mi" pattern is a line/space/line pattern. The last time they read this song they saw a space/line/space "sol-sol-la-la-sol-mi" pattern.)*

- Clap the rhythm of the words while singing the song with the Italian text.

- **Share the English translation of "Girogirotondo" with the children:**

  'Round and 'round the circle,
  See how wonderful the world is,
  Look at the ground, let's all fall down.

- *Children all over the world sing this song and play the singing game we are about to play.*

"Girogirotondo" *Continued*

- **Play a Game:** Invite the children to form a circle while holding hands.

- Tell them this song is like "Ring Around the Rosie." *You will get to fall gently to the floor during the last phrase.*

- Sing the song while walking counterclockwise in the circle to the macrobeat. Make the tempo slower at the end of the third measure (on the word "terra") and fall to the floor during the last phrase.

 Ask the children to point their toes to be ready to take the first step in the correct direction before you ask them to walk in the circle.

 "Jim Along Josie"

STRAND: Perform: *Sing, Play*

- *This song is called "Jim Along Josie."* Teach the song by rote. **CD 9:6** **CD 9:7**

- Prepare D and A on the Orff instruments or resonator bells. Invite two (or more if instruments are available) children to play one of the quarter-note bordun patterns.

- Sing the song with the bordun accompaniment.

 The term "bordun" is part of the Orff Method. It is an open fifth interval (a drone).

- Select new children to play the instruments and sing/play.

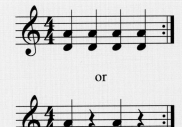

or

LESSON 32

Jim Along Josie

TRADITIONAL
Arranged by ROBERT W. SMITH

Hey, Jim a-long, Jim a-long, Jo-sie,

hey, Jim a-long, Jim a-long Joe. Hey, Jim a-long, Jim a-long, Jo-sie,

hey, Jim a-long, Jim a-long Joe. *Face to your part-ner, hand on your knees,*

clap three times and turn a-round please.

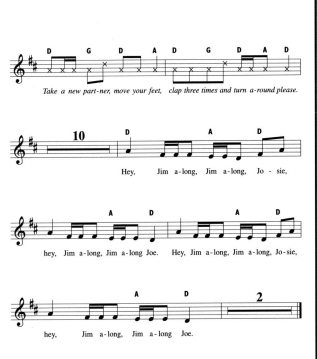

Take a new part-ner, move your feet, clap three times and turn a-round please.

Hey, Jim a-long, Jim a-long, Jo-sie,

hey, Jim a-long, Jim a-long Joe. Hey, Jim a-long, Jim a-long, Jo-sie,

hey, Jim a-long, Jim a-long Joe.

③ *"Jim Along Josie"* Continued

Progress Preview

What:

Are the children consistently demonstrating the steady beat?

How:

1. As the children prepare to perform the bordun for "Jim Along Josie," tell them that those who are not playing the instruments should pat their laps to the steady beat.

2. *As you show the steady beat, I will write how you do.* Explain they will earn a plus if they show the steady beat consistently and a half plus if they do not.

3. As the children perform, observe their ability to maintain the steady beat and mark the PR1 accordingly.

 Teacher Note Most should be demonstrating the steady beat consistently by now.

MARKING THE PR1:

+ = demonstrates the steady beat
| = does not demonstrate the steady beat

④ ## "Over in the Meadow"

STRAND: Perform: *Sing, Play*

- **Big Book:** Sing "Over in the Meadow" and point to the animals on page 62.

  CD 9:8
  CD 9:9

- Invite the children to sing the song again and copy your movements:

  1. **First phrase:** Tap the macrobeat:
  Over in the meadow in the sand in the sun,

  2. **Second phrase:** Tap the macrobeat:
  Lived an old mother turtle and her little turtle one.

  3. **Third phrase:** Clap the rhythm of the words:
  "Dig," said the mother, "I dig," said the one.

  4. **Last phrase:** Tap the macrobeat:
  And they dug and were happy in the sand in the sun.

- Review the difference between the rhythm of the words and the steady beat.

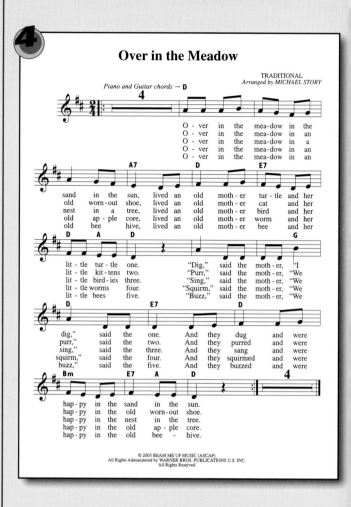

Over in the Meadow

TRADITIONAL
Arranged by MICHAEL STORY

Piano and Guitar chords → D

O - ver in the mea-dow in the
O - ver in the mea-dow in the
O - ver in the mea-dow in a
O - ver in the mea-dow in an
O - ver in the mea-dow in an

sand in the sun, lived an old moth-er tur-tle and her
old worn-out shoe, lived an old moth-er cat and her
nest in a tree, lived an old moth-er bird and her
old ap-ple core, lived an old moth-er worm and her
old bee hive, lived an old moth-er bee and her

lit - tle tur - tle one. "Dig," said the moth-er, "I
lit - tle kit-tens two. "Purr," said the moth-er, "We
lit - tle bird-ies three. "Sing," said the moth-er, "We
lit - tle worms four. "Squirm," said the moth-er, "We
lit - tle bees five. "Buzz," said the moth-er, "We

dig," said the one. And they dug and were
purr," said the two. And they purred and were
sing," said the three. And they sang and were
squirm," said the four. And they squirmed and were
buzz," said the five. And they buzzed and were

hap - py in the sand in the sun.
hap - py in the old worn-out shoe.
hap - py in the nest in the tree.
hap - py in the old ap - ple core.
hap - py in the old bee - hive.

④ **Corresponding Big Book page 62**

"Dig," said the moth-er, "I dig," said the one.

4 *"Over in the Meadow"* Continued

- **Big Book:** Ask the children to look at page 62. Read and clap the rhythm of the phrase "'Dig,' said the mother, 'I dig,' said the one." *Is this the steady beat or the rhythm of the words?* (Rhythm of the words)

- Sing all five verses and perform the tapping/clapping movements.

 Singing all five verses and demonstrating the difference between steady beat and rhythm of the words will prepare the children to play this pattern with the rhythm sticks.

- Distribute rhythm sticks and perform the tapping/clapping patterns with the rhythm sticks.

- Collect the instruments.

FINISH THE LESSON

 ## Recap

- *Today we sang songs and played instruments to show the rhythm of the words and the steady beat.*

- Sing and clap the phrase "'Dig,' said the mother, 'I dig,' said the one" from "Over in the Meadow." *Did I just perform the rhythm of the words or the steady beat?* (Rhythm of the words)

Pause to Think

- *This year in music we have really worked hard to know the difference between the steady beat and the rhythm of the words in our songs.*

- *How do you know the difference?*

- *What do you listen for or do to help you know the difference?*

6 *"Goodbye Song"*

STRANDS: Perform: *Move*; Respond/Reflect: *Listen*

 Teacher Note "Goodbye Song" was introduced in Lesson 1.

CD 9:10
CD 9:11

- Close the lesson by playing the recording of the "Goodbye Song." Invite the children to shake hands with their neighbor to the steady beat of the music.

- *As you did with the "Hello Song," let the music tell you when to turn and shake hands with the person on your other side. Provide an oral cue if the children do not switch at the end of each phrase of the music.*

> **LESSON EXTENSIONS**
>
> **Read** *Over in the Meadow* by John Langstaff, illustrated by Feodor Rojankovsky.
>
> Harcourt Trade Publishers. 1989.
>
> Sing the story using the traditional tune.

32

LESSON

LESSON SNAPSHOT

OBJECTIVES:
- The student will demonstrate vocal pitch accuracy on "sol-la-sol."
- The student will identify several Grade 1 core vocabulary words: steady beat, rhythm, melody, phrase, bar line, and repeat sign.

CONTENT	PURPOSE	ACTIVITY	BIG BOOK PAGE #	MEDIA CD*/DVD†	TRACK
"Hello Song"	Focus the lesson	Sing		**CD 9**	**12, 13**
Recording Progress: "Hi There, Hey There"	Summative, structured experience assessment	Demonstrate vocal pitch accuracy on "sol," "mi," and "la" during "Hi There, Hey There" Teacher listens and records		**CD 9**	**14**
DVD: Recording Progress: Vocabulary	Summative, structured product assessment	Identify core vocabulary words Teacher observes and records		**DVD 1**	**8**
"Goodbye Song"	Close the lesson	Sing		**CD 9**	**15, 16**
Interpreting the Results: The Development of Vocal Pitch Accuracy in Grade 1	Interpret scores	Review PR1			
Interpreting the Results: Vocabulary Identification	Interpret scores	Review worksheets			

* Tracks shown in green indicate accompaniment tracks. Tracks shown in red indicate practice tracks. These differentiated learning tracks are recorded at a slower tempo to help at-risk and special-needs learners with singing, movement, and language. These are explained within the lessons.

† The DVD is also available in VHS format.

TEACHER REFLECTIONS

_____

_____

CONCEPTS

Contrasts (vocal pitch accuracy)
Groups/Categories (vocabulary identification)

NATIONAL STANDARDS

- NS1 (Singing)

CRITICAL THINKING

- Core Thinking Skills:
  Observing, Encoding, Recalling, Representing, Identifying Attributes and Components, Identifying Relationships and Components

- Bloom's Correlation:
  Knowledge, Comprehension, Application, Analysis

- Critical Thinking Process:
  Comparison and Contrast

- Response Type:
  Verbal, Discussion

- Lesson Content Target:
  Two Types (modes) of Assessment

- Thinking Direction:
  Reflection, Metacognition

MUSIC FOR LIFE CATEGORIES

- Music for Beginnings
- Music for the End of the Day

CURRICULUM CONNECTIONS

- Language Arts

VOCABULARY

- Composer (review)
- Downward (review)
- Drum (review)
- Repeated Tone (review)
- Rest (review)
- Solo (review)
- Tempo (review)
- Upward (review)

ASSESSMENT 1

- Type:
  Summative, Structured Experience

- Assessable Component:
  Technical Musical Skill Development—
  Vocal Pitch Accuracy

- Assessment Response Mode:
  Performance

- Tool:
  Observation

- Scoring Guide:
  Bi-level, Single Criterion

- Criterion:
  The student sings accurately on the pitches on A, B and F#

- Levels of Achievement:
  + = demonstrated
  I = not demonstrated

ASSESSMENT 2

- Type:
  Summative, Structured Product

- Assessable Component:
  Vocabulary

- Assessment Response Mode:
  Responding

- Tool:
  Observation, Scoring

- Scoring Guide:
  0–3 = Novice
  4–5 = Developing
  6–7 = Proficient

LIFE SKILLS

- Stay on Task
- Follow Directions
- Think for Yourself

MATERIALS

- Worksheet #11 (Assessment):
  "Can You Identify the Vocabulary Words?"*
- DVD
- PR1*

*Worksheets and the Progress Record are found in the *Teacher Support Pack.*

EXPRESSIONS

Who hears music, feels his solitude; Peopled at once.

—Robert Browning

CONCEPTS

Contrasts (vocal pitch accuracy)
Groups/Categories (vocabulary identification)

FOCUS THE LESSON

1 *"Hello Song"*

STRAND: Perform: *Sing*

Teacher Note "Hello Song" was introduced in Lesson 1 and is also shown in Lesson 29.

 CD 9:12
CD 9:13

- Ask the children to join hands in a circle as they sing the "Hello Song."

- *This is a special day in music class.* Tell the children they are going to show you: (1) how well they can sing "sol," "la," and "mi" in a favorite song from earlier in the year, and (2) how well they know the words they have used all year in music.

DEVELOP THE LESSON

2 *"Hi There, Hey There"*

Teacher Note "Hi There, Hey There" was introduced in Lessons 5 and 17.

CD 9:14

Recording Progress

What:

Does the child demonstrate vocal pitch accuracy on "sol," "mi," and "la" during the singing of "Hi There, Hey There" ("do" = D)?

How:

1. *We learned the song "Hi There, Hey There" earlier this year. We are going to sing it today so you can show me how much you have improved your singing of "sol," "la," and "mi."*

2. Review the "Hi There, Hey There" song from Lesson 17 with the class:

   Hi there, hey there. We're so glad you came.

   Hi there, hey there. Will you say your name?

   My name is _____. We're so glad you came.

   Your name is _____. Now we know your name.

Recording Progress Continues

212

---

2 *"Hi There, Hey There"* Continued

Recording Progress Continued

Hi there, hey there. We're so glad you came.
s | s | m | s | s | l | s-m

Hi there, hey there. Will you sing your name?
s | s | m | s | s | l | s-m

My name is _____. We're so glad you came.
s | l | s-m | s | s | l | s-m

Your name is _____. Now we know your name.
s | l | s-m | s | m | r | m | d

---

3. **Play the Game:** Review the procedure for playing the game.

   Line 1: All sing, following your direction to look at one child.

   Line 2: All sing to child.

   Line 3: Child sings name. You and others respond.

   Line 4: All sing to child.

4. Tell the children that you are going to listen to their singing on "sol," "la," and "mi" (A, B, and F#) during the game. You will give them three marks of plus (+) or half plus (|), one for each pitch "sol," "mi," and "la." Show the children the PR1.

5. *In order to receive a plus for each pitch, you should sing like this.* Demonstrate the "My name is…" phrase. Ask the children to all sing this phrase together, inserting their own names where appropriate and singing as accurately as possible. Provide clarification as necessary, and make any corrections.

6. *You will receive a half plus if your singing is off pitch like this.* Demonstrate singing the "My name is…" phrase off pitch. This can be creative and funny if you desire. Ask the children to deliberately sing this phrase off pitch.

Teacher Note Asking the children to sing the phrase deliberately off pitch reinforces the concept of "on pitch."

7. *Now it is time to begin the assessment.* They will play the game starting with one child in the circle (determined by you) and going around the circle from child to child until everyone has sung.

Teacher Note As the assessment is proceeding, it is advisable to play a simple improvised bordun accompaniment on the piano during phrases 1 and 2 in order to keep the class on pitch. **Suggested accompaniment:** an open fifth, D-A, or a simple broken triad played with one hand.

8. Proceed with the game and mark the PR1 accordingly. Make a note of any behavioral characteristics that might result in off-pitch singing—shyness, posture, lack of attention, etc., and include these comments on the PR1.

 Teacher Note There will be three markings per child.

Recording Progress (Vocabulary)

Recording Progress

What:

Can the children identify several core vocabulary words they have learned this year in music class?

DVD 1:8

How:

1. Prepare the children for this worksheet assessment by getting them organized in the classroom in a manner that separates them.

Teacher Note One way to do this is to have the children sit in rows, "in their own space." It is also useful to have a seating chart for these types of activities.

2. **Worksheet #11:** Distribute pencils and the worksheet, one per child. Instruct the children to place these items on the floor in front of them until further instructed.

Teacher Note A music book serves as a good "lap desk" for this exercise.

3. *You are going to see Mr. Art, Maestro, Largo, and Cadenza. Listen very carefully because Mr. Art and his friends will tell you what to do on your worksheets.* Make a final check for supplies, worksheets, spacing, and names at the top; complete any unfinished preparation.

4. Turn on the DVD, and monitor the assessment. When the DVD is completed, collect the pencils and papers.

5. Score the worksheets, and enter the scores on the PR1.

Teacher Note **Answers to Worksheet #11:**
Practice 1—square—**tempo**
Test 2—circle—**repeated tone**
Test 3—heart—**drum**
Test 4—oval—**rest**
Test 5—half circle—**upward**
Test 6—diamond—**downward**
Test 7—triangle—**solo**
Test 8—star—**composer**

Corresponding Worksheet #11

First Grade Lesson 33
Worksheet #11 (Assessment)

Name _____

Classroom Teacher _____

Can You Identify the Vocabulary Words?

Let's Practice!

1. ☐   tempo

Let's Do!

2. ◯   drum

3. ♡   rest

4. ◯   upward

5. ◗   downward

6. ◇   repeated tone

7. △   composer

8. ☆   solo

FINISH THE LESSON

4 Recap

- *Today we sang "Hi There, Hey There" and matched pitches on "sol," "la," and "mi" as closely as possible.*

- *Mr. Art and his friends helped us review many of the words we have learned in music class this year.*

Pause to Think

- *You showed what you know in music by singing in a game and by drawing lines to words you know on a vocabulary worksheet.*

- *Which is your favorite way to show what you know? Why?*

5 *"Goodbye Song"*
STRAND: Perform: *Sing*

Teacher Note "Goodbye Song" was
introduced in Lesson 1.

CD 9:15
CD 9:16

- Close the lesson by inviting the
children to sing the "Goodbye Song"
with the recording.

6 **Interpreting the Results**

**THE DEVELOPMENT OF VOCAL
PITCH ACCURACY IN GRADE 1**

- When this assessment is completed, you will
be able to compare these markings with
those you made in Lesson 17 (mid-year).

- Look for improvement (moving from | to +)
or unchanged marks (| or +).

- Unchanged + markings are exactly what you
hope each child receives, because these
marks demonstrate consistent vocal pitch
accuracy on these pitches.

- Unchanged | markings need to be
interpreted carefully in terms of vocal
development. If the child appears to be
participating in the game to the best of his
or her ability but is still off pitch, this is
likely a developmental vocal control issue
and should correct itself with maturity and
future instruction.

- The same interpretation and procedures
hold true for children who reversed their
markings from mid-year to year-end—going
from + to |. If there are no inhibiting
behaviors noted during the game, this might
also be a developmental vocal control issue.
Close observation and assistance in Grade 2
is recommended.

6 **Interpreting the Results**
Continued

VOCABULARY IDENTIFICATION

- This test is designed so that most children
score in the proficient range. This is not a
true vocabulary test since the children are
not asked to either spell or define the terms.
They are only asked to recognize these in
print by drawing lines between these words
and shapes they already know.

- Children who score in the developing and
proficient range on this identification test
are ready to bring these words into their
vocabulary in Grade 2, where they will be
called upon to write the words and use
them in written responses.

- Children who score in the novice range on
this test will need to be observed closely in
Grade 2 and given assistance with
vocabulary recognition.

- There are several possible reasons for a
novice score:

  1. The child does not recognize the words.
  (The child could be new to your program
  or have a cognitive deficiency that
  impedes recognition.)

  2. The child does not understand this type
  of test. (The child may be unable to follow
  the directions or keep up, or perhaps there
  is a language problem.)

  3. The child's behavior during the test
  prevented him or her from completing
  the test in an accurate manner.

- You can determine the reasons for a
novice score by examining the PR1 and
the behavioral data you have gathered
throughout the year. Observations from,
and conferences with, parents and
classroom teachers are also good
sources of information.

LESSON SNAPSHOT

OBJECTIVES:
- The student will notate "sol-mi" and "sol-la-sol" on lines and spaces.
- The student will demonstrate aural discrimination.

CONTENT	PURPOSE	ACTIVITY	BIG BOOK PAGE #	MEDIA	
				CD*/DVD†	TRACK
Hand Drum and "sol-mi" Greeting	Focus the lesson Move to steady beat Sing "sol-mi"	Move Sing			
DVD: "What I've Learned in Music This Year" #1	Summative, Structured Product: Notation Assessment: "sol-mi" and "sol-la-sol" on lines and spaces	Notate "sol," "la," and "mi" on lines and spaces Teacher observes and records		**DVD 1**	**9**
DVD: "What I've Learned in Music This Year" #2	Summative, Structured Product: Aural Discrimination Assessment: Steady Beat versus Rhythm of the Words	Discriminate between steady beat and rhythm of the words Teacher observes, listens, and records			
"Goodbye Song"	Sing with Mr. Art and friends from DVD	Sing		**CD 9**	**17, 18**
Interpreting the Results: Notation	Interpret scores	Review worksheets			
Interpreting the Results: Aural Discrimination of Steady Beat and Rhythm of the Words	Interpret scores	Review PR1			

* Tracks shown in green indicate accompaniment tracks. Tracks shown in red indicate practice tracks. These differentiated learning tracks are recorded at a slower tempo to help at-risk and special-needs learners with singing, movement, and language. These are explained within the lessons.

† The DVD is also available in VHS format.

TEACHER REFLECTIONS

INSTRUCTIONAL FRAMEWORK

NATIONAL STANDARDS

- NS1 (Singing)
- NS6 (Listening)
- NS5 (Reading and Notating)

CRITICAL THINKING

- Core Thinking Skills:
  Observing, Encoding, Recalling, Representing, Identifying Attributes and Components, Identifying Relationships and Components

- Bloom's Correlation:
  Knowledge, Comprehension, Application, Analysis

- Critical Thinking Process:
  Metacognition

- Response Type:
  Verbal, Discussion

- Lesson Content Target:
  Two Types (modes) of Assessment

- Thinking Direction:
  Reflection, Metacognition

MUSIC FOR LIFE CATEGORIES

- Music for the End of the Day

CURRICULUM CONNECTIONS

- Language Arts

VOCABULARY

- Rhythm (review)
- Steady Beat (review)

ASSESSMENT 1

- Type:
  Summative, Structured Product

- Assessable Components:
  Theoretical, Notation: "sol," "mi," "la" on Lines and Spaces

- Assessment Response Mode:
  Responding

- Tool:
  Observation; Scoring

- Scoring Guide:
  0 = Novice
  1–2 = Developing
  3 = Proficient

ASSESSMENT 2

- Type:
  Summative, Structured Product

- Assessable Components:
  Fundamental Aural Discrimination, Same/Different, Steady Beat— Rhythm of the Words

- Assessment Response Mode:
  Responding

- Tool:
  Observation; Scoring

- Scoring Guide:
  0–1 = Novice
  2–3 = Developing
  4–5 = Proficient

LIFE SKILLS

- Stay on Task
- Follow Directions
- Think for Yourself

MATERIALS

- Hand Drum
- Worksheet #12 (Assessment): Notation*
- Worksheet #13 (Assessment): Steady Beat or Rhythm of the Words?*
- Pencils
- DVD
- PR1*

*Worksheets and the Progress Record are found in the *Teacher Support Pack.*

EXPRESSIONS

As poetry is the harmony of words, so music is that of notes.

—John Dryden

FOCUS (vertical)

FOCUS THE LESSON

1 Hand Drum and "sol-mi" Greeting
STRAND: Perform: *Sing, Move*

- Play a steady beat on the hand drum as class begins. *Put the steady beat in your feet with as little sound as possible.*

> **Teacher Note** If the children are entering the music room from the hall, having them walk to a steady beat is a good way to focus them as they enter.

- Walk the children to their seats as you continue to play the steady beat. The children who are seated should transfer the steady beat to their laps, patting the beat quietly.

- Once the children are seated, stop the beat. Ask them to prepare their hand sign for "sol" and greet them as follows, using hand signs:

  Your Greeting:
  Hel-lo boys and girls
  s   m   s   s   m
  ta   ta   ti-ti   ta

  Children's Response:
  Hel-lo (your name)
  s   m   s   s   m
  ta   ta   ti-ti   ta

- *This is a special day. Today you will show me how much you have learned in music this year.*

- *Mr. Art and his friends are going to join us on a DVD.*

DEVELOP THE LESSON

2 "What I've Learned in Music This Year"

- Prepare the children for today's two worksheet assessments by getting them organized in the classroom in a manner that separates them, if you have not already done so.

DVD 1:9

> **Teacher Note** Suggestions for organizing the children for their assessments are in Lesson 33.

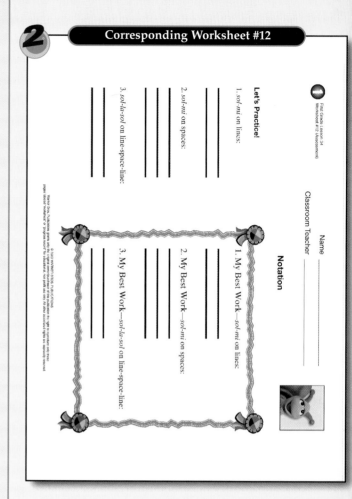

2 Corresponding Worksheet #12

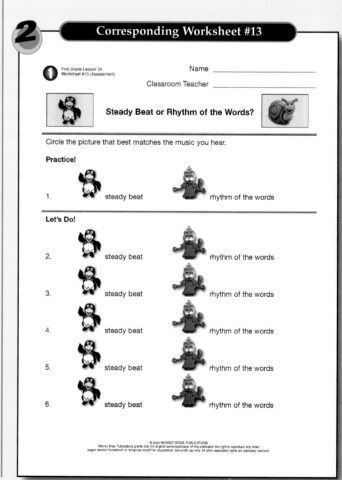

2 Corresponding Worksheet #13

First Grade Lesson 34
Worksheet #13 (Assessment)

Name _____
Classroom Teacher _____

Steady Beat or Rhythm of the Words?

Circle the picture that best matches the music you hear.

Practice!

1.   steady beat   rhythm of the words

Let's Do!

2.   steady beat   rhythm of the words

3.   steady beat   rhythm of the words

4.   steady beat   rhythm of the words

5.   steady beat   rhythm of the words

6.   steady beat   rhythm of the words

Music Expressions

"What I've Learned in Music This Year" *Continued*

- **Worksheets #12 and #13:** Distribute pencils and both worksheets, one set per child. Instruct the children to place these items on the floor in front of them until further instructed.

- *Today you are going to watch Mr. Art, Maestro, and Cadenza. Mr. Art and his friends will tell you what you need to know about completing your worksheets. Make a final check for supplies, worksheets, spacing, and names at the top. Complete any unfinished preparation.*

- **Play the DVD:** Monitor the assessment during the DVD. When the DVD is completed, collect the pencils and papers.

3 Recording Progress

Recording Progress

What:

Can the children write "sol-mi" and "sol-la-sol" on lines and spaces? **DVD 1:9**

Can the children aurally distinguish steady beat and the rhythm of the words?

How:

1. Follow the DVD instructions.

2. **Worksheets #12 and #13:** When the DVD ends, collect the worksheets.

3. Score the worksheets and enter the scores on the PR1.

 Teacher Note
Answers to Worksheet #13:
Practice 1—**steady beat**
Test 2—**steady beat**
Test 3—**rhythm of the words**
Test 4—**rhythm of the words**
Test 5—**steady beat**
Test 6—**rhythm of the words**

4. Both sheets should be scored according to the scoring guides presented in the frameworks below, and the results should be entered on the PR1.

Scoring Guide:
0 = Novice
1–2 = Developing
3 = Proficient

Recording Progress Continues

3 Recording Progress *Continued*

Recording Progress Continued

5. A response should be counted as correct when the entire pattern is correctly and clearly placed on the lines or spaces as instructed.

6. You should not expect the children's notes to be "perfect"—they are most likely to be oddly shaped or bumpy due to their developing muscle control of the pencil.

7. What you are looking for is the location of the note on the staff—line or space or the combination for "sol-la-sol."

Scoring Guide:
0–1 = Novice
2–3 = Developing
4–5 = Proficient

FINISH THE LESSON

Recap

- *Today you showed what you know in music by writing music and listening for the difference between the steady beat and the rhythm of the words.*

- *How did you know you were making the right choices on your worksheets?*

"Goodbye Song"
STRAND: Perform: *Sing*

 Teacher Note "Goodbye Song" was introduced in Lesson 1. **CD 9:17** **CD 9:18**

- *Close the lesson by inviting the children to sing the "Goodbye Song" along with Mr. Art and his friends from the DVD.*

Interpreting the Results

NOTATION

- This test is designed so that most children should score in the proficient range. The practice opportunity is provided to help the children be more confident in their writing before they are asked to place answers in the boxes.

- Children who score in the developing and proficient range on this identification test are ready to continue notation at the Grade 2 level, where they will begin to put melodic and rhythmic values together.

- Children who score in the novice range on this test will need to be observed closely in Grade 2 and given assistance in understanding what line notes and space notes are.

- There are several possible reasons for a novice score:

  1. The child does not know the difference between line and space notes yet. (The child could be new to your program or have a cognitive deficiency that impedes this understanding.)

  2. The child does not understand this type of test. (The child may be unable to follow the directions or keep up, or perhaps there is a language problem.)

  3. The child is not yet able to use a pencil efficiently.

  4. The child's behavior during the test may have prevented him or her from completing the test in an accurate manner.

- You can determine the reasons for a novice score by examining the PR1 and the behavioral data you have gathered throughout the year. Observations from, and conferences with, parents and classroom teachers are also good sources of information.

 Interpreting the Results
Continued

AURAL DISCRIMINATION OF STEADY BEAT AND RHYTHM OF THE WORDS

- This test is designed so that most children score in the proficient range. The songs chosen as examples for rhythm of the words are readily recognizable at this time of the year and rhythmically active, in discernible contrast to the steady beat.

- Children who score in the developing and proficient range on this test are ready to bring these skills to Grade 2, where they will be developed in their study of musical patterns.

- Children who score in the novice range on this test will need to be observed closely in Grade 2 and given as much additional practice with aural discrimination as possible.

- There are several possible reasons for a novice score:

  1. The child does not recognize the words. (The child could be new to your program or have a cognitive deficiency that impedes recognition.)

  2. The child does not understand this type of test. (The child may be unable to follow the directions or keep up, or perhaps there is a language problem.)

  3. The child's behavior during the test prevented him or her from completing the test in an accurate manner.

- You can determine the reasons for a novice score by examining the PR1 and the behavioral data you have gathered throughout the year. Observations from, and conferences with, parents and classroom teachers are also good sources of information.

34

LESSON

LESSON SNAPSHOT

OBJECTIVE:	• The student will perform core songs from Grade 1 that include rest, repeated tone, singing, speaking, steady beat, and melody patterns.

CONTENT	PURPOSE	ACTIVITY	BIG BOOK PAGE #	MEDIA CD*/DVD†	TRACK
"Hey There, Neighbor"	Identify repeated tones Speak and sing Play game	Sing Speak Move Teacher observes and listens		CD 9	19, 20
"Head and Shoulders, Baby"	Sing and identify repeated tones Identify and perform rests	Sing Move		CD 9	21, 22
"Sally Go 'Round the Sun"	Sing and identify repeated tones and phrases Sing and sign melody patterns "sol-mi-do," "sol-la-sol," and "mi-re-do"	Sing Sign Read	29	CD 9	23, 24
"Over in the Meadow"	Sing and follow animal listening map Sing and play rhythm of the words and steady beat	Sing Play	6	CD 9	25, 26
"You're a Grand Old Flag"	Sing and sign repeated tones on "do" March to the steady beat Sing and sign "sol-mi-do"	Sing Move Sign		CD 9	27, 28
Favorite Song Sing-Along: "Bluebird" "Star Light, Star Bright" "This Old Man"	Build basic repertoire	Sing		CD 9 CD 9 CD 9	29 30 31

* Tracks shown in green indicate accompaniment tracks. Tracks shown in red indicate practice tracks. These differentiated learning tracks are recorded at a slower tempo to help at-risk and special-needs learners with singing, movement, and language. These are explained within the lessons.

† The DVD is also available in VHS format.

TEACHER REFLECTIONS

_____

_____

_____

_____

_____

INSTRUCTIONAL FRAMEWORK

NATIONAL STANDARDS

- NS1 (Singing)
- NS2 (Playing)
- NS5 (Reading and Notating)
- NS6 (Listening)
- NS9 (Understanding Relationships)

CRITICAL THINKING

- Core Thinking Skills:
  Observing, Recalling, Identifying Attributes and Components, Classifying, Identifying Relationships and Patterns

- Bloom's Correlation:
  Knowledge, Comprehension, Application, Analysis

- Critical Thinking Process:
  Metacognition

- Response Type:
  Verbal, Discussion

- Lesson Content Target:
  Songs Reviewed in This Lesson, Music Vocabulary

- Thinking Direction:
  Reflection, Metacognition

MUSIC FOR LIFE CATEGORIES

- Music for Movement
- Music to Remember
- Music for National Pride

CURRICULUM CONNECTIONS

- Language Arts

VOCABULARY

- Drum (review)
- Melody (review)
- Metal (review)
- Repeated Tone (review)
- Rest (review)
- Singing Voice (review)
- Speaking Voice (review)
- Steady Beat (review)
- Wood (review)

LIFE SKILLS

- Make Eye Contact
- Include Others
- Take Turns
- Make Choices

MATERIALS

- Big Book
- Assorted Wood Instruments
- Assorted Metal Instruments
- Hand Drums

EXPRESSIONS

A nation creates music—the composer only arranges it.

—Mikhail Glinka

FOCUS THE LESSON

1 "Hey There, Neighbor"

STRAND: Perform: *Sing, Chant, Move*

- Invite the children to sing "Hey There, Neighbor" and perform the actions they learned earlier in the year.

 CD 9:19 **CD 9:20**

Teacher Note The song and actions for "Hey There, Neighbor" were introduced in Lesson 3. As the students perform and identify repeated tones in the following songs, watch for those who may be having difficulty. Assist as necessary.

- **Play a Game:** *As we perform "Hey There, Neighbor" this time, we will play a partner game and add these words: "Find another partner, move along. Say their name before we sing this song."*

- *Sometimes I will ask you to speak your partner's name. Other times I will ask you to sing it.*

- *Raise your hand if you can tell us how speaking and singing are different.*

- Sing the song and play the game.

DEVELOP THE LESSON

2 "Head and Shoulders, Baby"

STRAND: Perform: *Sing, Move*

- *You are going to hear a song you learned early this year—"Head and Shoulders, Baby." Invite the children to clap their own hands on 1, 2, and 3 and touch their own chests on the rests between the numbers.* Play the recording.

 CD 9:21 **CD 9:22**

Teacher Note "Head and Shoulders, Baby" was introduced in Lesson 6.

- Help the children find partners. *Tap your partner's hands on the numbers and touch your own chest on the silent beats.* All sing the song and perform the partner actions.

- *Raise your hand if you remember what the silent beat between the numbers is called.* (Rest)

- *When you sing and perform the song with your partner this time, instead of touching your own chest on the rests, show the rest sign.* (Palms up)

Hey There, Neighbor

Adapted and Arranged by
ROBERT W. SMITH

Hey there, neigh-bor, what do you say?__ It's gon-na be a hap-py day!__

Greet your friends and boo-gie on down.__

Give 'em a bump__ and turn a-round.__

spoken
Hey there, neigh-bor, move a-long.__ Can you

find a new part-ner 'fore I fin-ish my song?__

Hey there, neigh-bor, what do you say?__

It's gon-na be a hap-py day!___

Greet your friends and boo-gie on down.__

Give 'em a bump__ and turn a-round.__

Head and Shoulders, Baby

African-American Game Song

1. Head and shoul - ders, ba - by, one, two, three. Head and shoul - ders, ba - by, one, two, three. Head and shoul - ders, head and shoul - ders, head and shoul - ders, ba - by, one, two, three. (2.) Hips and thighs,___ ba - by, one, two, three.

2. Hips and thighs, baby,...
3. Knees and ankles, baby,...
4. Ankles and toes, baby,...

Sally Go 'Round the Sun

AMERICAN FOLK SONG
Arranged by MICHAEL STORY

f Sal - ly go 'round the sun, Sal - ly go 'round the moon, Sal - ly go 'round the chim - ney pot ev - 'ry af - ter - noon. Sal - ly go 'round the sun, Sal - ly go 'round the moon, Sal - ly go 'round the chim - ney pot ev - 'ry af - ter - noon.

"Head and Shoulders, Baby"
Continued

- *Do the pitches for "one, two, three" move upward, downward, or stay the same? (Stay the same)*

- *What do we call pitches that stay the same? (Repeated tones)*

"Sally Go 'Round the Sun"

STRANDS: Perform: *Sing*; **Read/Notate**

- **Big Book:** Show the melody map from Lesson 15 of "Sally Go 'Round the Sun" on page 29. *This map shows the melody of a song we know. Raise your hand if you can sing the song.* CD 9:23 CD 9:24

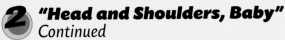 "Sally Go 'Round the Sun" was introduced in Lesson 15.

- Invite the child who recognized the song to trace the melody map on the Big Book page as everyone sings "Sally Go 'Round the Sun."

- *How many phrases are in "Sally Go 'Round the Sun"? (Three)* Remind the children the form of the phrases is short-short-long.

"Sally Go 'Round the Sun"
Continued

- *You know all the signs for this song.* Review the "sol-la-sol" pattern, "sol-mi-do," and "mi-re-do."

- Invite the children to sing and sign "Sally Go 'Round the Sun" with you.

"Over in the Meadow"

STRAND: Perform: *Sing, Play*

- **Big Book:** Invite the children to sing "Over in the Meadow" as they follow the animal listening map of the song on page 6. CD 9:25 CD 9:26

 The "Over in the Meadow" song and listening map were introduced in Lesson 4. The music is repeated in Lesson 32 on page 208.

- Distribute assorted wood and metal instruments, along with a few hand drums to half the class. Ask the children to identify whether they have received a wood or metal instrument, or a drum. *How do you know?*

"Over in the Meadow" *Continued*

- **Big Book:** *As we sing "Over in the Meadow" this time, if you have an instrument, play it on the steady beat of verses 1, 2, and 4. On verse 3, stop playing so those without instruments can clap the rhythm of the words.*

  Teacher Note The children performed the steady beat and rhythm of the words in Lesson 32.

- When the children have sung, played, and clapped their parts on "Over in the Meadow," ask those with instruments to pass them to the other children. Repeat, switching parts.

 "You're a Grand Old Flag"
STRANDS: **Perform:** *Sing, Move;* **Connect**

- Invite the children to stand and sing "You're a Grand Old Flag." *As we sing with the recording, let's march in place to the steady beat.*

  CD 9:27
  CD 9:28

  Teacher Note "You're a Grand Old Flag" was introduced in Lesson 6 as a listening example.

 "You're a Grand Old Flag"
Continued

- Sing the words "grand old flag." *Do these pitches move upward, downward, or stay the same?* (Stay the same) *We sing these repeated tones on "do." Raise your hand if you remember the sign for "do." All practice singing "grand old flag" while signing "do, do, do."*

  Teacher Note The children added the "do" sign to this song in Lesson 12.

- Sign "sol-mi-do-do-do." *What words of the song "You're a Grand Old Flag" did I just sign?* ("You're a grand old flag") *All practice singing and signing this pattern.*

- Ask the children to sing "You're a Grand Old Flag," signing the solfège patterns they have learned.

FINISH THE LESSON

Recap

- *Today we sang several songs we learned this year in music class.*

- *What songs did we sing today? ("Hey There, Neighbor," "Head and Shoulders, Baby," "Sally Go 'Round the Sun," "Over in the Meadow," and "You're a Grand Old Flag")*

Pause to Think

- *Which of these songs is your favorite? Why?*

- *Be sure to use some of our music vocabulary in your answer.*

Favorite Song Sing-Along

STRAND: Perform: *Sing*

- **Close the lesson by inviting the children to select one or two songs from the following list of songs to sing:**
  - "Bluebird"
  - "Star Light, Star Bright"
  - "This Old Man"

CD 9:29
CD 9:30
CD 9:31

 The children review most of the Grade 1 core songs in Lessons 35 and 36.

LESSON SNAPSHOT

OBJECTIVES:
- The student will perform core songs from Grade 1 that include singing, steady beat, rhythm of the words, melody direction, and music symbols.
- The student will respond through mirroring to musical phrases.

CONTENT	PURPOSE	ACTIVITY	BIG BOOK PAGE #	MEDIA CD*/DVD†	TRACK
"Sakura"	Mirror through movements Identify phrases	Mirror Teacher observes		CD 9	32
"Star Light, Star Bright"	Sing and sign "sol-mi-sol-mi" Perform rhythm of the words and steady beat Sing and clap ostinato Chant and clap ostinato	Sing Sign Chant		CD 9	33, 34
"Rig-a-Jig-Jig"	Perform walking beats and skipping beats Play singing game to reinforce steady beat and rhythm of the words	Sing Move		CD 9	35, 36
"This Old Man"	Sing and sign "sol-mi-sol" Review "sol-mi" line note rule Review "sol-mi" space note rule	Sing Sign Review		CD 9	37, 38
"Yankee Doodle"	Perform rhythm of the words and steady beat Review bar line, double bar line, and repeat sign	Sing Perform Review	38 40	CD 9	39, 40
Favorite Song Sing-Along: "Did You Feed My Cow?" "You're a Grand Old Flag" "Over in the Meadow"	Build basic repertoire	Sing	62 63 64	CD 9 CD 9 CD 9	41 42 43

* Tracks shown in green indicate accompaniment tracks. Tracks shown in red indicate practice tracks. These differentiated learning tracks are recorded at a slower tempo to help at-risk and special-needs learners with singing, movement, and language. These are explained within the lessons.

† The DVD is also available in VHS format.

TEACHER REFLECTIONS

INSTRUCTIONAL FRAMEWORK

NATIONAL STANDARDS

- NS1 (Singing)
- NS6 (Listening)
- NS8 (Making Connections)

CRITICAL THINKING

- Core Thinking Skills:
  Observing, Recalling, Identifying Attributes and Components, Classifying, Identifying Relationships and Patterns

- Bloom's Correlation:
  Knowledge, Comprehension, Application, Analysis

- Critical Thinking Process:
  Metacognition

- Response Type:
  Verbal, Discussion

- Lesson Content Target:
  Songs Reviewed in the Lesson, Music Vocabulary

- Thinking Direction:
  Reflection, Metacognition

MUSIC FOR LIFE CATEGORIES

- Music for National Pride
- Music From Many Nations
- Music to Remember
- Music for Moving
- Music for Fun and Imagination

CURRICULUM CONNECTIONS

- Language Arts

VOCABULARY

- Bar Line (review)
- Double Bar Line (review)
- Line Note (review)
- Phrase (review)
- Repeat Sign (review)
- Space Note (review)
- Steady Beat (review)
- Upward/Downward (review)

LIFE SKILLS

- Make Eye Contact
- Take Turns
- Accept Role and Responsibility
- Stay on Task

MATERIALS

- Big Book

EXPRESSIONS

There is always one moment in childhood when the door opens and lets the future in.

—Graham Greene

CONCEPTS   Contrasts *(culminating)* Groups/Categories *(culminating)*

FOCUS THE LESSON

1 *"Sakura"*

 STRANDS: Perform: *Move,* Respond/Reflect: *Listen;* Connect

- *Mirror me as I move to "Sakura."* Your movements should be slow and smooth like the phrases of the music.

CD 9:32

Teacher Note The mirroring/phrasing activity for "Sakura" was introduced in Lesson 9. As the children mirror your movements during "Sakura," watch for those having difficulty.

- *Each of my movements matched a musical idea of the music. What do we call a musical idea?* (Phrase)

DEVELOP THE LESSON

2 *"Star Light, Star Bright"*

STRAND: Perform: *Sing, Chant*

- Invite the children to sing "Star Light, Star Bright."

CD 9:33
CD 9:34

Teacher Note "Star Light, Star Bright" was introduced in Lesson 15.

- Sign "sol-mi-sol-mi." *Which words of the song did I just sign?* ("Star light, star bright")

- All sing and sign the "sol-mi-sol-mi" patterns as they occur within the song.

- Clap the rhythm of the words, "Star light, star bright, first star I see tonight." *What words of the song did I clap? How did you know?*

- Invite the children to chant and clap "Star Light, Star Bright."

- Repeat, singing the song instead of chanting.

- Remind the children of the "star light, star bright" ostinato pattern they learned earlier in the year.

  1. All chant and clap the ostinato.
  2. All sing and clap the ostinato.

2 *"Star Light, Star Bright"* Continued

- Divide the class in two parts and instruct one half to sing the song while the other half sings the "star light, star bright" quarter-note ostinato.

- Switch parts.

3 *"Rig-a-Jig-Jig"*

STRAND: Perform: *Sing, Move*

- Invite the children to sing "Rig-a-Jig-Jig." Remind them there is a walking section and a skipping section. *On the walking section, show me how your hands "walk" on your legs. Make them "skip" on your legs on the skipping section.*

CD 9:35
CD 9:36

Teacher Note "Rig-a-Jig-Jig" was introduced in Lesson 24.

- All sing the song while walking and skipping with hands on legs. *We're going to learn a new game for "Rig-a-Jig-Jig."*

- **Play the Game:** Ask the children to form a standing circle. To begin, you are "It."

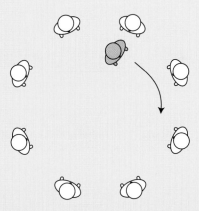

1. "It" walks to the steady beat on the inside of the circle. The children in the circle patsch their knees to the steady beat as they sing.

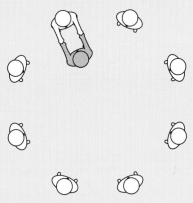

2. "It" stops and faces a person in the circle. The partners hold hands and push/pull arms to the rhythm of the words "rig-a-jig-jig." They swing arms from side to side on the macrobeat of "away they go, away they go, away they go." Repeat.

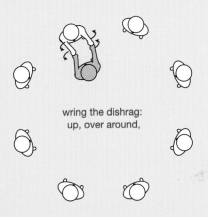

wring the dishrag:
up, over around,

3. At the end of Section B ("Hi ho, hi ho, hi ho") "It" and his or her partner "wring the dishrag."

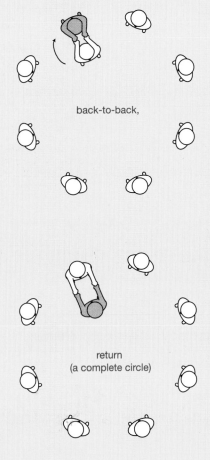

back-to-back,

return
(a complete circle)

4. The first "It" takes his or her partner's place in the circle. The new "It" begins walking around inside the circle as the children begin the song again.

- Demonstrate the push/pull motions for "rig-a-jig-jig." *Did my hands move to the steady beat or the rhythm of the words?* (Rhythm of the words) *How do you know?*

3

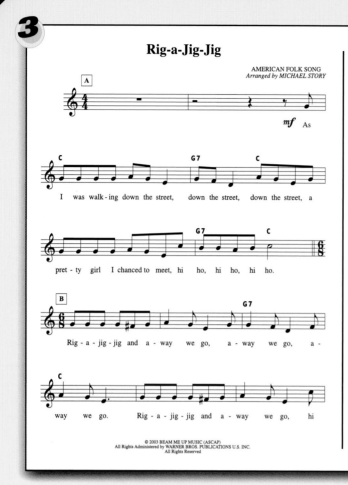

Rig-a-Jig-Jig

AMERICAN FOLK SONG
Arranged by MICHAEL STORY

"This Old Man"

STRANDS: Perform: *Sing*;
Read/Notate

- All sing "This Old Man" with
  the recording.

  CD 9:37
  CD 9:38

- **Teacher Note** "This Old Man" was
  introduced in Lesson 10.

- Sign "sol-mi-sol" in the rhythm of the words
  "this old man, he played one." *Which words
  of the song did I just sign?* ("This old man, he
  played one") *How could you tell?*

- *As we sing the song this time, sign the
  "sol-mi-sol" pattern every time it occurs.*
  All sing and sign.

- *Does the "sol-mi-sol" pattern move upward,
  downward, or both?* (Both)

- *When we learned "This Old Man," we wrote
  "sol-mi-sol" on the staff. Raise your hand if you
  can sing the rule when "sol" is on a line.* (When
  "sol" is on a line, "mi" is on the line below)
  All sing the rule to review line notes.

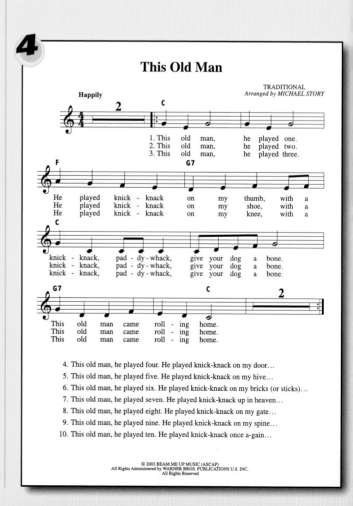

This Old Man

TRADITIONAL
Arranged by MICHAEL STORY

Happily

1. This old man, he played one.
2. This old man, he played two.
3. This old man, he played three.

He played knick-knack on my thumb, with a
He played knick-knack on my shoe, with a
He played knick-knack on my knee, with a

knick-knack, pad-dy-whack, give your dog a bone.
knick-knack, pad-dy-whack, give your dog a bone.
knick-knack, pad-dy-whack, give your dog a bone.

This old man came roll-ing home.
This old man came roll-ing home.
This old man came roll-ing home.

4. This old man, he played four. He played knick-knack on my door…
5. This old man, he played five. He played knick-knack on my hive…
6. This old man, he played six. He played knick-knack on my bricks (or sticks)…
7. This old man, he played seven. He played knick-knack up in heaven…
8. This old man, he played eight. He played knick-knack on my gate…
9. This old man, he played nine. He played knick-knack on my spine…
10. This old man, he played ten. He played knick-knack once a-gain…

4 *"This Old Man"* Continued

- *Raise your hand to sing the rule when "sol" is on a space. (When "sol" is on a space, "mi" is on the space below) All sing the rule to review space notes.*

5 *"Yankee Doodle"*
STRAND: Perform: *Sing*

- Invite the children to sing "Yankee Doodle" while patsching the steady beat.

CD 9:39
CD 9:40

"Yankee Doodle" was introduced in Lesson 19 and is repeated in Lesson 28.

- **Big Book:** Ask the children to look at page 38 from Lesson 19. Point to the following symbols and ask them to explain each:
  - Bar line
  - Double bar line

Bar line and double bar line were introduced in Lesson 19. Repeat sign was introduced in Lesson 20. Review Big Book page 40 to see the repeat sign.

- Clap the rhythm of the words of Section A without singing the song. *Did I clap the rhythm of the words or the steady beat? (Rhythm of the words) How could you tell?*

- Ask the children to sing the song again. *This time, clap the rhythm of the words on the first part, and patsch the steady beat on the second part.*

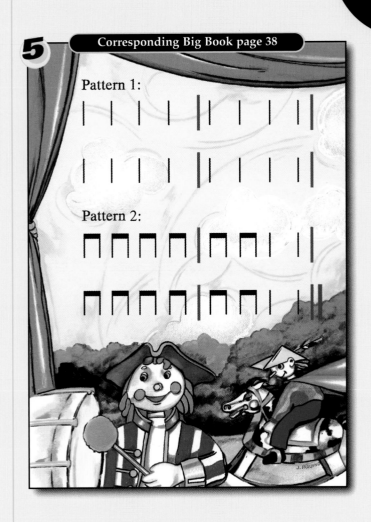

Corresponding Big Book page 38

Pattern 1:

Pattern 2:

Corresponding Big Book page 40

FINISH THE LESSON

6 Recap

- *Today we sang songs we have learned in music class this year.*

- *What songs did we sing?* ("Star Light, Star Bright," "Rig-a-Jig-Jig," "This Old Man," and "Yankee Doodle")

- *We began today's lesson by mirroring phrases to "Sakura." What is a phrase?* (Musical idea)

Pause to Think

- *What did you like best today? Why?*

- *Be sure to use some of our music vocabulary in your answer.*

7 Favorite Song Sing-Along

STRAND: Perform: *Sing*

- Close the lesson by inviting the children to select one or two songs to sing from the following list:

  CD 9:41
  CD 9:42
  CD 9:43

  - "Did You Feed My Cow?"
  - "You're a Grand Old Flag"
  - "Over in the Meadow"

Teacher Note The children have reviewed most of the Grade 1 core songs in Lessons 35 and 36.

- **Big Book:** *Let's look at pages 63 and 64 and say "Goodbye" to our music friends.* Review their names with the children. (Mr. Art and Cadenza)

Corresponding Big Book page 62

"Dig," said the moth-er, "I dig," said the one.

Corresponding Big Book page 63

Goodbye

Corresponding Big Book page 64

Photo: Donald Notsworthy

Music Expressions

Music Notes

Music Notes

Music Notes

Music Notes

Music Notes

Music Notes

Glossary

First Grade Core Words

bar line
The vertical line placed on a staff to divide the music into measures

bells
A hollow, usually cup-shaped metallic instrument that makes a ringing sound when struck

chant
Text spoken rhythmically

composer
A person who writes music

cymbals
A musical instrument made of two brass plates that are clashed together to make a sharp, ringing sound

double bar line
Two vertical lines placed on the staff to indicate the end of a section or a composition

downward
Melodic direction toward lower sounding pitches

drum
A musical percussion instrument usually consisting of a hollow cylinder with a thin layer of skin or plastic stretched over one or both ends that is played by striking

fast
Quick; moving with great speed

high
Sounds that are high in pitch

jingle bells
A hollow, usually round metallic instrument that makes a ringing sound when shaken

line note
A musical symbol with a staff line through its center

loud
A high volume of sound

low
Sounds that are low in pitch

lullaby
A song to quiet children or lull them to sleep

march
Music with a strong steady beat for marching

melody
A series of musical phrases that express a composer's thoughts

metal
A category of instruments whose sound is made by the striking of metal parts

pattern
The order of pitches or rhythms

phrase
A musical thought or idea

repeat sign
The symbol that is two dots and a double bar line indicating to repeat a section or a composition

repeated tone
A tone that occurs more than once

rest
The symbol for a silent unit of time

rhythm
The organization of sound and silence in time

rhythm sticks
A wooden instrument that is two sticks played by striking one upon the other

singing voice
The voice we use when we sing songs

slow
Unhurried; not fast

soft
Quiet, little volume

solo
One person performing alone, with or without accompaniment

space note
A musical symbol written between staff lines

speaking voice
The voice we use when we are talking

steady beat
The pulse of music

tempo
The speed at which music is performed

upward
Melodic direction toward higher sounding pitches

wood
A category of instruments whose sound is made by the striking of wooden parts

woodblock
A wooden instrument that is a block played by striking the block with a mallet

Index